Presented to:

_____

From:

_____

Date:

_____

WORDS OF PRAISE FOR
TAKE IT TOO FAR

"This book provides believers with a timely tool for today's generation of women. It's easy for us to look to the right and the left and feel that we're either doing too much or not enough for God's kingdom. Or worse yet, there's a nagging fear that whatever it is we put our hand to, we're doing it wrong. Jess has a beautiful way of pointing us back to the gospel and making it simple to live out in today's world. Her words remind us that our purpose on earth is simply to partner with the work already completed on the cross. In the same way that we can walk in freedom thanks to God's gift of Jesus, we can also walk in humility thanks to God's gift of the Holy Spirit. Thanks, Jess, for teaching us the both-ands of following Jesus. *Take It Too Far* will ignite women of God, and also provide a fresh presentation of the Good News to the lost."

—Rach Kincaid, writer and Bible teacher

"*Take It Too Far* is an incredible resource for those who are tired of holding back. Abundant Life, Boundless Love, Unending Grace—yes! We need all those things! This isn't a time in culture when we can play small or sit on our hands. It's time for us to take it too far, and Jess leads us straight to the heart of the matter."

—Alli Worthington, bestselling author of *Fierce Faith*

"I think of Jess Connolly as some sort of firework-sunflower who tells the truth and gets you on your feet. I love that she is honest and inspiring in her writing. I love that she's faithful and intentional about how she teaches the Bible. And I love that she makes me want to give her a hug. I love her newest work, *Take It Too Far*, and I know you will, too."

—Scarlet Hiltibidal, author of *Afraid of All the Things*

"What an incredible thing to fix our thoughts and actions on . . . these attributes of God in us that we can take too far! That means we can't be too much when it comes to the qualities outlined in this devo—love, joy, peace, and patience. I am so thankful for this devotional to fix my attention on the areas where I can live in freedom with no limits!"

—Katie Walters, CEO of Francis + Benedict

"Jess Connolly's friendship and teaching always leave me more in love with Jesus. With compassion and unwavering conviction, Jess offers a desperately needed invitation to quit playing it safe and take God at His word, trusting His character and believing that we are who He says we are. Beautifully written and theologically sound, *Take It Too Far* is not merely Jess's theory . . . it's her heartbeat. Don't miss out on the transforming truth waiting for you in these pages!"

—Nicole Zasowski, marriage and family therapist
and author of *From Lost to Found*

"We serve an outrageous God. He is a creative genius, a brilliant visionary, an infinite lover, and an unrelenting strength. We could spend our whole lives plumbing the depths of our Father, but too often we are content to sit on the seashore. Not Jess Connolly. Jess understands that when our vision of God is small, our faith and our lives will be too. In these pages, Jess dares us to lean in and out, further than we ever have before, and just see what God will do. I sincerely hope you will join her."

—Sharon Hodde Miller, author of *Nice: Why We Love to Be Liked and How God Calls Us to More*

"This is not just another devotional. Jess takes us back to the foundations of our faith and helps us rehearse the pillars so that we can run wholeheartedly—with full confidence in what God has called us to do—into our missions. What I love most is the real-life applications that accompany each devo and that we get the gift of clear and concise practicals with a bit of 'fire' that only Jess can give. Even here, her voice and heart shine through along with her unwavering desire to see each of us live just a little more freely. This is exactly what my soul needed."

—Kennesha Buycks, author and owner, Restoration House

"If there's more to know about God's heart, mind, and ways, I'm the girl who wants to be first in line, in all the way, and the one who wants to know! This book is going to tear down every wall we've built under the influence of limiting beliefs. For one hundred days, get ready to stretch wide your heart, renew your mind, refresh your soul, and get lost in the extravagant love of our limitless God. Like the healthiest of Enneagram eights, Jess will challenge us to push out farther, into the deep, while taking herself there too. Read this book if you agree that it's time stop playing small or keeping things safe by letting God's word take us further into the reality of His kingdom; further than we ever thought we could go!"

—Alisa Keeton, author of *The Wellness Revelation* and *Heir to the Crown*, and founder of Revelation Wellness®

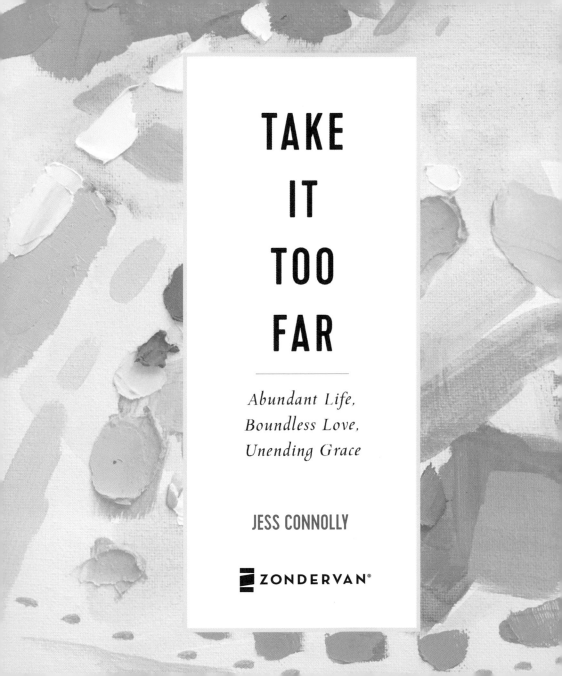

TAKE
IT
TOO
FAR

Abundant Life,
Boundless Love,
Unending Grace

JESS CONNOLLY

ZONDERVAN®

ZONDERVAN

Take It Too Far

© 2020 by Jessica Ashleigh Connolly

Requests for information should be addressed to:
Zondervan, 3900 Sparks Dr. SE, Grand Rapids, Michigan 49546

ISBN: 978-0-3100-9558-3

All Scripture quotations, unless otherwise indicated, are taken from The Holy Bible, New International Version®, NIV®. Copyright © 1973, 1978, 1984, 2011 by Biblica, Inc.® Used by permission of Zondervan. All rights reserved worldwide. www.Zondervan.com. The "NIV" and "New International Version" are trademarks registered in the United States Patent and Trademark Office by Biblica, Inc.®

Scripture quotations marked CSB are taken from The Christian Standard Bible. Copyright © 2017 by Holman Bible Publishers. Used by permission. Christian Standard Bible®, and CSB® are federally registered trademarks of Holman Bible Publishers, all rights reserved.

Scripture quotations marked ERV are taken from the Easy-to-Read Version (ERV). Copyright © 2006 by Bible League International.

Scripture quotations marked ESV are taken from the ESV® Bible (The Holy Bible, English Standard Version®). © 2001 by Crossway, a publishing ministry of Good News Publishers. Used by permission. All rights reserved.

Scripture quotations marked MSG are taken from *The Message*. Copyright © by Eugene H. Peterson 1993, 1994, 1995, 1996, 2000, 2001, 2002. Used by permission of NavPress. All rights reserved. Represented by Tyndale House Publishers, Inc.

Scripture quotations marked NASB are taken from the New American Standard Bible®, Copyright © 1960, 1962, 1963, 1968, 1971, 1972, 1973, 1975, 1977, 1995 by The Lockman Foundation. Used by permission. (www.Lockman.org)

Scripture quotations marked NKJV are taken from the New King James Version®. © 1982 by Thomas Nelson. Used by permission. All rights reserved.

Scripture quotations marked TPT are taken from The Passion Translation®. Copyright © 2017 by BroadStreet Publishing® Group, LLC. Used by permission. All rights reserved. (thePassionTranslation.com)

Any Internet addresses (websites, blogs, etc.) and telephone numbers in this book are offered as a resource. They are not intended in any way to be or imply an endorsement by Zondervan, nor does Zondervan vouch for the content of these sites and numbers for the life of this book.

Published in association with literary agent Jenni Burke of D.C. Jacobson & Associates LLC, an Author Management Company. www.dcjacobson.com.

Interior design: Emily Ghattas
Cover painting by Joanna Posey

Printed in China

20 21 22 23 24 DSC 10 9 8 7 6 5 4 3 2 1

CONTENTS

FOREWORD

I know I have a unique ability. One might even call it a superpower.

I find myself taking things I shouldn't take too far, *very* far. And the things I should take too far in life, not very far at all.

Have you ever noticed this unique superpower in your life?

Coffee drinking, let's take it too far! Water. . . . Isn't coffee basically water?

Sports! Let's watch *all* the football today! (For some, this could be the equivalent of taking Anthropologie's 40-percent-off sale too far.)

How much ice cream is too much ice cream?

But what about the things of God? I find myself obsessing over pretty-natural things yet not obsessing over the supernatural things of God. What about the beautiful and abundant life God has for me in the kingdom? What about the things he has called me to and purposed for me to take too far?

"God what's the minimum I can do today?"

"God, how can I do just enough to ensure that blessing in my life?"

"God what's the appropriate church attendance to make sure my life runs smoothly?

"How can I love people at a minimum?"

I don't know who you are, and I don't know where you're from, but I know who you belong to. You and I have been created by the God of the universe to take all of His good and wonderful things too far in the life He's given us.

I didn't always view life this way, which is why I'm so grateful God gave me Jess. I love marriage because it has the ability to take who you are and make you more like the beautiful person you've been created to be. My marriage to Jess has accomplished this in all the best ways.

God knew I needed someone to help me take the things of the kingdom too far. He knew I needed someone who would encourage me to run hard after the abundance God purposed for me in and through Jesus. God knew I needed someone kind enough to tell me, "Don't take that too far," and "Here! Take this too far! I see God's hand on your life! Take it and run with it!"

The same gift God gave me, He now gives to you.

Enclosed in this book, you'll find one hundred encouragements from my best friend to you, proclaiming from the rooftops to take it too far. Whether it's God-given rest, seeing the Father's heart for justice established in your neighborhood, dancing with your friends and family, or even vulnerability, Jess is here to let you know you can never take the amazing and beautiful things of God too far.

And even though her desire to encourage you to take it too far is great, all she wants for you is to fall more in love with the God who fearfully and wonderfully made you.

Friends, because of this, I know this book will be a gift to your life. And as this book becomes a gift to your life, I know God will continue to make you a gift to this world as you join with Him in taking it too far.

Nick

INTRODUCTION

Friends! I am so excited and hopeful for the 100-day journey you and I are about to embark on.

A few years ago, I came across this verse, and it emboldened and encouraged my spirit:

> Enlarge the place of your tent, stretch your tent curtains wide, do not hold back; lengthen your cords, strengthen your stakes. (Isaiah 54:2)

Reading those words, I couldn't help thinking about all the times I play it safe in life, in love, in work, in all the good things—for a variety of reasons. Maybe it's fear; maybe it's because I'm trying to fit in with the culture around me, but I wonder two things when I think about playing it safe:

1. What would happen if God had played it safe, just played the middle of the road when it came to loving and redeeming the lives of His kids?

2. What if the real reason I hold back in so many good things is because I've forgotten that I'm made in the image of my passionate, loving, wild, and good God?

We're going to look at one hundred terms that relate to our walk with God. Some of them are attributes of our heavenly Father. Others are descriptions of what God's people can look like, qualities we can possess by the power of God. We're going to ask this honest question of our own souls: What would it look like if we took these beautiful and godly attributes too far in our own lives? What would it look like if we agreed with our actions, with our hearts, and with our lives that we were meant to be like Him?

Let's dive in, asking Him to stretch the curtains of our hearts wide so we can see where we've been holding back. Let's ask Him to lengthen and deepen the cords of truth in our lives as we learn more about Him, His character, His love, and His power. And let's ask Him to strengthen the stakes of conviction in our souls, so we can head out into the world, ready to take our roles as ambassadors too far.

You ready? I can't wait.

Let's go.

JESS

1 PEACE

You will keep in perfect peace those whose minds are
steadfast, because they trust in you.—Isaiah 26:3

"You will keep . . . in perfect peace . . . those whose minds are steadfast, . . . because they trust in you."

I say it slowly over and over again as I fall asleep because I am worried.
I am scared. My husband has had an issue with his throat for months—
and it's gotten increasingly worse. He's been to the doctor a handful of
times, but he has an appointment with a specialist tomorrow to have a
scope done. I feel sure they're going to find something awful. In this
moment I'm wondering:

*Do I believe that God will keep me in perfect peace if I keep my thoughts
on Him?*

*Do I believe that God will keep me in perfect peace if this doctor's appoint-
ment goes badly tomorrow?*

*Do I believe that perfect peace is available to me if the one I love the most
is taken from me?*

And that's when I hear the Holy Spirit whisper, *"Take the promise
of peace too far."* I realize that my mind is not actually on God at all; it's
centered on fear. So I start praying and thanking Him for His presence.

I begin acknowledging how good and faithful He's always been to me, even when the world has seemed harsh. I even take it so far as to remember and recount: *I wouldn't love this husband so much if it weren't for God's grace, and I certainly wouldn't be married to him if the power of my Father's reconciliation weren't active and at work in my life.*

And then, without reciting anything, I drift off to sleep. Because my mind is stayed on God and I've remembered that He is trustworthy. The next day the doctor's appointment goes surprisingly well—but I know it's not because I've willed it to be so. And peace has had its work in my heart once again, so I'm ready for the next disruption. And this is for you as well, this continual work of peace that holds us and prepares us for the next moment, the next day, the next opportunity to worship with faith.

Take Peace Too Far

How can you choose peace today? Take a moment to think about what you know to be true about your situation versus what the world is telling you right now.

2 REST

Don't you know he enjoys giving rest to those he loves?—Psalm 127:2 msg

Can we take rest too far?

What if we become slothful?

What if we stop working?

What if we neglect all God has given us to do?

Maybe the question isn't, Can we take rest too far? Maybe the question is, Are we actually resting? I'd love to propose that true rest will restore and revive us to a place where we are eager and itching to use what we've got for God's glory and the good of others. True rest and restoration won't slow us down but will help us swing so far into His presence and pleasure that we're filled up to swing out into productivity once again.

But I'm learning I often confuse hiding and rest. Hiding puts on headphones and tries to forget the world; rest leaves me restored and hopeful. Hiding says I need to be away from others so I can be safe, while rest reminds me that only the gospel brings me safety. Hiding leaves me scared to get up, and rest knows I was made to move.

Hiding says, "Just give me a break!" and rest says, "Come away with me; come learn unforced rhythms of grace." Can you take rest too far?

I vote no. But are you actually resting? Only you can know that. God is never disappointed in your rest, but rather, I believe He wants to meet you there. It's the desire of His heart to put you back together, to restore your soul, to comfort and repair what has been worn out, and to send you out in His grace once again.

Take Rest Too Far

This one is so fun! Rest today! Just do it. Ten minutes or two hours or half the day. Rest and ask God to help you to do it for His glory.

3 ENCOURAGEMENT

Therefore encourage one another and build each other
up, just as in fact you are doing.—1 Thessalonians 5:11

The Greek word for "encourage" here is *parakaleo*, and it essentially means "to call to, exhort, summon, entreat, comfort and even console." But the word is a root of *parakletos*, which has legal overtones, and really broken down it means to advocate personally for someone. It's a word of exhortation that would stand up for the soul of someone in God's court.

Encouragement isn't just speaking kind words or saying nice things; it's testifying on each other's behalf, both among ourselves as Christians and to the spiritual forces that come against us. When we encourage, when we speak life, and when we admonish those we're close to, we're standing between them and the literal enemy of their souls and testifying to God's capacity and love for them.

Why do people deserve our encouragement? Because our Father loves them, sent His Son for them, and values their lives even at the cost of His own. And because no matter what has happened between us in the human world, we share an eternal enemy in Satan—the accuser and liar who has an individualized attack plan for every person we love.

We get to take encouragement too far because it's how we're uniquely wired to fight for one another against darkness and discouragement. But we shouldn't be scared to take it too far because we lose nothing in the process. With every word of encouragement spoken, we only validate and agree further with the truth that God has written over our lives: we're encouragers, we're warriors, and we're testifiers of truth.

Let's take it too far and encourage others often and with fervor.

Take Encouragement Too Far

Before your head hits the pillow tonight, encourage someone else. Tell them you're proud of them; tell them you see God moving in and through them; tell them He's going to give them what it takes to win!

4 ADVENTURE

"Call to me and I will answer you and tell you great and unsearchable things you do not know."—JEREMIAH 33:3

The most adventurous thing I ever did was go cave diving in Mexico. Friend, I was terrified. My husband *loves* adventure. When it's just the two of us (he doesn't love putting our kids in danger), he loves to take off and do something that makes his heart beat faster. I've never felt like I'm in a truly dangerous situation, because he loves me and wants good for me, but my body, mind, and soul perceive adventure as danger.

And so, this one time, we found ourselves cave diving. We had life jackets, a tour guide, lamps for when the caves got too dark, and breathing gear—everything we needed to execute this small amount of adventure in a safe way—but I still could not get my heartbeat to a reasonable rate for the entire time. Everyone else was immersing their heads deep beneath the surface of the water, using their gear to see all they could. I, in contrast, kept my hands gripped tightly around my life jacket, with my head above water, where I could access oxygen without anyone's help.

If it were up to me, left to what I know and what I'm comfortable with, I'd probably live out the rest of my days in a pretty standard and rhythmic pattern. I'd wear mostly the same clothes and keep the same routines, I don't know that I'd ever get on another plane, and I definitely wouldn't go cave diving.

But something has happened to me that keeps me pushing outside the limits of what feels comfortable, and that's the truth that I get to see more of God when I go outside the boundaries of my life. When I follow His voice, His call to places outside my comfort zone, I get to see the light of His love in new and fresh ways; I get to see adventure.

Because I said yes to something that felt incredibly uncomfortable, for just a few moments I got to experience what God was doing and growing and tending to *underwater* in Mexico. I got to see rocks that He'd created and beauty He'd crafted; essentially, I got to see more of Him.

We have a choice every single day: to stay where we are, with what we're used to, or to follow God's voice to adventure. Let's take it too far today and see what else He's got to show us.

Take Adventure Too Far

Only you know what's comfortable for you and what's adventurous. Maybe the most adventurous thing you could do today is to go to God and ask Him where He wants to take you *today* and follow where He leads.

5 DANCING

Break forth with dancing! Make music and sing God's
praises with the rhythm of drums!—Psalm 149:3 TPT

I had a hard time getting into college because I didn't do so well in high
school. But there was one school that seemed to be interested and open
to me attending—a small, private Christian college. I thought nothing could be better than combining my extreme love for Jesus with my
problem of no other colleges wanting me, so I set my sights on this school
and jumped in with both feet. I did the whole weekend tour thing, where
they let you come and stay in the dorm and see what college life is like. I
loved it! Suddenly I could picture myself there!

Because it was a Christian college, there were some rules, but they
weren't intimidating to me. No drinking. Cool. I'd already done that in
high school and gotten it out of my system. You had to be in your dorm
by 9 p.m. *Sounds like someone is forcing me to be an introvert; I'm down!* But
then we got to the hardest rule of all . . . no dancing.

No dancing? I mean, I understand we can't bust a move in the cafete-
ria with the boys. But what about in my room alone? With my headphones
on? What about when I pass a test or want to celebrate a win with my
friend? Can I dance then? No. I'd have to sign a covenant to promise not

9

to dance. And so, even though I needed this college way more than they needed me, I had to say no. I left the tour weekend and never looked back.

I think there will be dancing in heaven. I know dancing is mentioned multiple times in Scripture, and I don't believe it's allegorical. After all, the Bible does say there's "a time to dance" (Ecclesiastes 3:4). I think that means not only us but God too. I believe that we get to move our bodies to music to agree with all sorts of things. We agree that we've been set free when we dance. We agree that there's hope when we dance. We agree that hard times aren't here forever when we dance.

I got into another college, thank God, and ended up hosting worship and dance nights in my dorm room. We'd read Scripture, worship a little, then turn up the tunes and turn down the lights and dance until we could barely stand up. And I'm kind of still doing that. I heard the Christian college changed their rules and you can dance now. Praise God.

Take Dancing Too Far
Dance today–and not metaphorically. Maybe
alone. Maybe grab a friend or one of your
kids. Dance and see what happens.

6 HONESTY

Do not lie to each other, since you have taken off your old self with its practices and have put on the new self, which is being renewed in knowledge in the image of its Creator.—COLOSSIANS 3:9–10

I realized I was way too honest as a child. My dad and I had a complicated relationship, as he lived overseas most of my life, and when he'd come home, my extreme honesty would get the better of me. I would say hurtful things about how he wasn't often around. I would blurt out my complicated and painful feelings, and even though it was more than thirty years ago, I can still picture his face as he'd sit, stunned, across from me.

So I swung back the other way and began hiding and lying about how I felt. Not only with others but also with myself. I'd bury my thoughts, ideas, and feelings deep down until even I had a hard time accessing them. Even if you just asked me what I wanted for dinner, I wasn't sure what to say because I didn't know if it was all right to be that honest.

Now I vacillate between the two practices—sharing exactly what I think and feel, and keeping my own true thoughts and feelings pretty tightly locked up. And depending on the day, you can encounter either version of me, though I try to rely on the Holy Spirit to know which side is needed in the moment.

Should we tell the whole truth and nothing but the truth all the time? Isn't that often hurtful? Yes, yes, it is. But surely we shouldn't lie—or put on pretenses. That can't be what God wants from us, can it? No, I don't think it is.

What Colossians 3 encourages me with is this: the knowledge that I've been made new and I've been renewed in the image of God, meaning I can access His wisdom and knowledge about how to be honest and how to also love others well.

I don't believe that taking honesty too far means we just say what we're thinking, feeling, or seeing every second of the day. I do think it means relying on God to help us to be honest and gentle and humble and wise, the way Jesus is all of those things at once too.

Take Honesty Too Far

Start today with being honest with God. Tell Him what you think, what you need, what you feel. He can take it, and He can help you be honest with others and yourself.

7 PRESENT

"Be alert, be present. I'm about to do something brand-new.
It's bursting out! Don't you see it? There it is! I'm making a road
through the desert, rivers in the badlands."—Isaiah 43:19 MSG

Have you felt it? The regret of leaving a place or even finishing a day and knowing you weren't really there? I have. I've left a party, filled with people I love, and felt the conviction in my soul that something else grabbed my mind or my affection when I wish the people there had received my attention. I'll remember seeing someone's face but feel the pain of not having spoken to him. Or I'll think I can remember a certain conversation where I asked someone how she was doing, but I won't recall the answer . . . because I wasn't fully present.

When this conviction comes, we've got three choices. We can make excuses for ourselves and get prideful, we can live in self-condemnation and feel like we're awful humans, or we can experience the regret and then repent. I believe that when we say we're sorry, even if it's just to God and ourselves, we'll feel the freedom of grace, and that will compel us to do better next time.

But why does it matter that we're fully present? Sometimes if I'm not careful, I'll trick myself into thinking it's only important that I'm present so I can love others well and give them my full attention. And then I'm guilted into being attentive just for their sake, and I miss out on so much that God has to offer.

See, I think being present is a great way to love others well, but more than that, it enables us to catch notice of what God is doing. We see growth and fruit in others when we pay attention, when we've slowed down enough to pause and ponder—then we can partner with the Holy Spirit to perceive what it is He's up to. We can catch the look of grief or sadness on someone's face, we can fight for them in prayer, and then we can experience the joy that comes when God relieves that person's pain.

When we pause to be more present, we're not just being kind and loving others well, but we're loving God well and loving ourselves by paying attention to where and how He's moving in our daily lives.

Take Being Present Too Far

Today identify three things that keep you from
being present and ask God to help you remove
those as barriers. For example, if it's electronics,
can you go a few hours phone-free? If it's fear,
can you ask God to help you walk in faith?

8 FAITH

God is our refuge and strength, an ever-present help in trouble.—Psalm 46:1

I struggle with fear. My fear has cropped up in some silly places and some standard places. About two years ago, after a really turbulent flight, I suddenly became terrified of flying. I've flown overseas many times, even as a little kid, but I found myself, as a thirtysomething who travels to teach, saying no to work and fun because the flights might be too long.

I'm tough! I'm wild! I'm a woman of faith! But catch me in the middle of a flight and you'll see a sad, scared crybaby, begging God to allow my fellow passengers and me to land safely. I have a hard time accessing feelings of faith when I'm right in the middle of feeling terrified.

I was telling my counselor today about my fear of flying, and she said something incredibly wise: "Somewhere along the way your brain learned that fear kept you safe on the plane. You got scared, and you got what you wanted—to land safely—so your brain decided subconsciously that the trick of being scared worked."

But my conscious, awake brain and my soul know better. They know that fear doesn't keep me safe; it keeps me caged. Fear isn't the safety net; it's the trap that keeps me from experiencing abundance and obedience.

I couldn't help but think of all the other places we might need to apply this fear-versus-faith analogy. Where and when did you learn that fear helped you survive and give up on faith helping you thrive? Maybe your subconscious learned a lesson incorrectly, and it's time to learn the truth. The best way I know to do that is to act courageously and experience the fruit for myself. My plan is to praise where I used to fear and teach my brain how well that works.

Let's take faith too far and teach our brains a lesson. Let's take faith too far and believe God will show up, He'll still be good, and He'll still be God—even when our bodies and the outside world tell us otherwise. Let's agree with our hands, our mouths, and our hearts that our Father is who He says He is and is worth putting our faith in. Let's remember that we're children of God and agree with the full lives of faith that have been purchased for us today.

Take Faith Too Far

Ask God to help you hear any moment today when
you stop trusting Him. Ask Him to give you eyes
to see and ears to hear exactly where you give in to
fear. Then step out in faith and confidence.

9 LISTENING

My dear brothers and sisters, take note of this: Everyone should be quick to listen, slow to speak and slow to become angry.—JAMES 1:19

Do you have a pet peeve? I have one that I'm not proud of. It's when you're talking to someone and they say a casual and dismissive "yeah, yeah, yeah" in the middle of your sentence. Do you know what I'm talking about? It's a sweet little affirmative gesture that's become commonplace among women of our generation. Maybe they're saying "Right!" or "Totally!" as you talk, but it's to affirm rather than interject.

One time I was talking to a friend, and she was doing the "yeah, yeah, yeah" as I spoke, and it struck a weird chord with me. So weird that I stopped midsentence and said, "Do you know what I'm about to say? I haven't finished the sentence. How can you say, 'Yeah, yeah, yeah'?" Because she's a normal human, she was taken aback by my directness and strangeness, and I realized how rude I sounded and told her how sorry I was. Hence, why I'm so embarrassed about my pet peeve.

But there's another reason I'm embarrassed. The reason that bothers me is because I perceive that I'm not being listened to, and that grieves me because I know I struggle with being a good listener. I'm just not the best listener. I struggle with interjecting, I sometimes get distracted when others are talking, and I can even talk, talk, talk for minutes on end without coming up for air to see how you are. And I'm not proud of it.

But isn't it so often true that we see our biggest weaknesses in others, and that makes us all the more tender to them? The reason I want to be a better listener is not because I don't want to frustrate others. The reason I want to be a better listener is not so I'll seem like I'm a good listener. The reason I want to be a good listener is because God our Father is a good listener, and I want to have every attribute of His that He's given me access to.

I know that I can listen well not only to other humans but also to God's voice. And I know that much of Scripture talks to the strength, grace, humility, wisdom, and power that come from just listening.

So I'm with you in this, sister, willing to take it too far, asking God to help me listen like He does. For His glory, the good of others, and the growth of my own soul. You in?

Take Listening Too Far

Start with God first. See if you can set aside just five or six minutes today to listen to God. See what He says to you, see what He shows you, and then take that same practice into your relationships with other people. You are a good listener. It's time to own that.

10 OBEDIENCE

[Jesus] replied, "Blessed . . . are those who hear
the word of God and obey it."—Luke 11:28

I stink at taking medicine sometimes. I'll have a headache for hours
before I remember that ibuprofen fixes that. I don't know if I forget or if
I'm just stubborn, but I often don't do what I know will help. And then
when I do it, I'm relieved and grateful. I walk around for an hour saying,
"I'm so glad my headache is gone!" And I'm shocked and blessed and
astounded that the tiny pills helped the way they always do.

Obedience is crazy in this same way because most of us know what
God is asking us to do on a daily basis. We know what is the healthy,
wise, uncomplicated decision that will help us experience Him more abundantly, live more freely, and love others better. I find that it's rare that we
don't know what God wants us to do and much more common that, for
whatever reason, we just don't do it.

Yet all of His Word and all of our past experience with Him point to
this one truth: when we act in obedience, even if it's hard, we feel better.
We experience blessing—even if it's not worldly blessing. We know that
He's no genie in a bottle who will make us rich if we read our Bibles every
day—He's so much better than that! He gives His power and peace and

abundance and healing and freedom—and Himself! He gives Himself! He blesses us for our obedience.

We just gotta take the step. Well, we don't "gotta," but we get to. Make the call. Open the Bible. Cancel the appointment. Call the friend. Walk to the neighbor's house. Tithe the money. Start the business. Turn off the TV. Take the nap. Drink the water. We get to obediently do what we know He's made us to do today, and then experience the thrill of abundance and blessing that come afterward.

So let's do it. Let's take obedience too far today, in small and big ways, because this is the beautiful cycle of faithfulness and blessing that we've been invited into. This is what we were made for.

Take Obedience Too Far

Write today's date and what you know God is asking you to do in obedience. Do it, and then come back later and write down some of the ways you perceive Him blessing you now that you've obeyed Him.

11 PATIENCE

You intended to harm me, but God intended it for good to accomplish what is now being done, the saving of many lives.—Genesis 50:20

The story of Joseph in the Bible has always been one of my favorites. You can find the whole tale starting in Genesis 37:1. If you're not familiar with the story of Joseph, here's a quick CliffsNotes version.

Joseph was the beloved son of Jacob. Joseph's older brothers resented his favor and the gift of vision that God had given him, so they plotted to kill him, but then let him off the hook and sold him into slavery instead.

A lot of painful and confusing things would happen in Joseph's life, but God continued to give him dreams and vision for how things would end up, and they ended up in his favor.

Every year I intently study Joseph's story to see what fresh thing God might have for me to see in this beautiful historical account. This year, one verse got me right in the gut: "When two full years had passed, Pharaoh had a dream" (Genesis 41:1).

At one point in Joseph's life, he was wrongfully accused of something and ended up in prison for two years, waiting for someone to remember him and have mercy on him. Two years of waiting. And that was on top of the number of years he'd already been suffering.

I know that because Joseph was human, those two years were hard and discouraging. I mean, he was in jail. But I also know that because of how he responded once God brought healing and restoration to his life, he could not have been writhing in bitterness and seething with frustration. There's one reason that Joseph might have been able to press through so much pain and hardship with patience: he was a man of great vision.

When we have a vision for where we're going, we can access all new levels of patience. And when you think about it this way, how can you be patient if you don't know what you're waiting on?

God may not give us every detail of what's going to happen to us. Let's thank Him that He won't! But I do believe He's personal and kind, and He will give us vision to help us access patience in every season and situation.

Let's take it too far and ask for vision so we can be patient people, just like Joseph.

Take Patience Too Far
Where is God asking you to be patient? Have
you asked Him for vision? Do that today.

12 POWER

But he said to me, "My grace is sufficient for you, for my power is made perfect in weakness." Therefore I will boast all the more gladly about my weaknesses, so that Christ's power may rest on me.—2 Corinthians 12:9

Do you want to live a powerful life? Man, I do. Power is ability. Power is capacity. Power is the supply we need to do what we want, to do what we need. Power is helpful. The world will tell us some very interesting ways to gain power. Some are logical, some not so much.

Get a good night's sleep and eat healthy foods.

Visualize what you want.

Step on other people to get where you want.

Be kind.

Trick people into thinking you're kind.

Earn a lot of money.

Spend a lot of money.

Use your strengths.

Subdue your weaknesses.

Hide your problems.

Fix your problems.

Be special.

Don't be too special.

It's kind of exhausting to keep up with all the ideas of how to gain and wield power according to the world. Yet the Word of God tells us a whole separate way: Be weak. Have weaknesses. Thank God that you have weaknesses, and let Him move in and through you so you can see, access, and be impacted by His power.

It makes sense to me for two reasons: every earthly plan to gain and use power is derived from pretending we're not weak, and that seems to lead to pain and failure for everyone. Jesus is the hero; we're just a part of the rescue plan—ambassadors placed here to help restore what He loves. So we might as well acknowledge our fallible places in the whole scenario.

Second, all earthly plans to gain and use power seem to end in using it for our own good, whereas the kingdom plan allows the power of God to rest on our lives so we can give God glory and work for the good of others. And that sounds like the kind of power that I want to partner with.

Take Power Too Far

Name one weakness that you've been trying to hide,
fix, or pretend doesn't exist. Ask God to help you
believe in His grace and goodness, and see what
happens when His power is made perfect.

13 WILD

Do not be conformed to this age, but be transformed by the renewing of your mind, so that you may discern what is the good, pleasing, and perfect will of God.—Romans 12:2 csb

God used a documentary about wild horses a few years ago to stir up my affections for women in our generation, and I wrote about it in my first book, *Wild and Free*. I was watching as these beautiful wild horses ran free on the banks of the North Carolina beaches, thinking about how they were so untamed, so uncivilized, and I longed to be like them.

At its worst, Christian culture can be a systematic process to make people just like us, to make them tame and seemingly safe. But Jesus came that we might be free, and He made us uniquely individual and different, so it seems incredibly sad that we'd want to strip any of His kids of the blessing of being who He made them to be. Yet it happens, and often I perceive my own complicity in the system that tries to make others tame.

I noticed it most about six years ago when we began to plant our church, Bright City. I had been working under an incredibly false assumption that the women who came to our church would be like me, would seek God like me, would hear from Him like me, and would respond to Him like me. As women came, bringing their full, vibrant selves to the table, I sensed the wildness among us, but my flesh responded in fear—thinking that different was dangerous.

God was trying to color my world, trying to paint complexity and beauty and mystery all over the way I interacted with Him. He was trying to bring me freedom and help me see just how wild He could be in the women around me. Thankfully, I saw the wild horses, and I remembered the pain of times that others had tried to contain or stifle Him in me, and I started on a quest to get back to the wild—not held down by cultural expectations or conclusions but freed up to be the wild woman He created me to be.

The world will tell us that wild is bad and dangerous, but God did not make us to fit into the trappings of society or the expectations of others. We can serve Him, follow Him, worship Him, and respond obediently to Him and still look dangerous to others. May we be women who take our wild freedom too far, for His glory and for the contagious catching on of freedom around us.

Take Being Made Wild Too Far

Identify one way you've conformed to the pattern
of this world instead of wildly obeying what God
has asked you to do. Repent and be free!

14 THOUGHTFUL

Live carefree before God; he is most careful with you.—1 Peter 5:7 MSG

My friend Kristen is the most thoughtful person, and she expresses it in a variety of ways, but one of my favorite things she does is write cards. About once a month or so, I'll look down on my seat at church to see a card from Kristen, and my whole face breaks out into a smile. They're never just short sentiments; they're thoughtful encouragements that I need right at that very moment. So you can imagine my extreme delight when I found out this one detail about the way Kristen writes cards:

She completely pre-writes each card by typing out what she wants to say and *then* hand writing the message God has placed on her heart. I feel thought of by God when I get her cards, not just thought of by Kristen. And there's something else interesting I've noticed about her card writing: she never expects cards back. She's just blessed to deliver a message of life and hope and good news.

I think Kristen can be so free of care for herself, and so full of thought for others, because she knows and lives as if God cares for her. She agrees with the truth that God is thoughtful, careful, and intentionally loving toward her, and she doesn't discount herself from those attributes.

Instead, she knows that because He is careful and thoughtful with her, she is freed up to be the same way for others.

For the longest time when I'd describe how thoughtful Kristen is, I'd immediately discount myself from the possibility that I could be just as caring. "I wish I could be that thoughtful!" "I wish I could be as intentional and caring as you are!" And then I realized that I was limiting God's power, love, and capacity to cause me to love others. And more than that, I was ignoring how thoughtful He was with me. Because when I'm compelled by His goodness and love and care, I can't help but extend that same intentionality—however it looks for me—to those I love.

You might not be meant to write cards; that may not be your thing. But you were absolutely created to be thoughtful, and you're freed up to care for others because God has been so kind, so careful, so intentionally thoughtful toward you.

Take Thoughtfulness Too Far

See if you can capture one way that God has been thoughtful toward you recently. How has He intentionally seen you, blessed you, held you? What does that make you want to do? Who in your life could use some thoughtful care today? Take it too far!

15 VULNERABLE

But we have this treasure in jars of clay to show that this all-surpassing power is from God and not from us.—2 Corinthians 4:7

A few years ago, I learned about the difference between transparency and vulnerability. They sound similar and may even look alike from the outside, but the motivation and the outcome for the two practices are different.

Transparency says, *I'll let you see through. No hiding; there are no barriers between you and my insides. I'll tell you what I'm thinking. I'll tell you what's in there. I'll show you stuff.* I am pretty good at being transparent; more than that, it comes naturally to me, and I often have to intentionally work at keeping things safe and hidden that need to be.

But vulnerability . . . that's different. Vulnerability is being woundable. It means that not only am I going to let you see me, but I'm going to open myself up to being hurt by you. Vulnerability means that I'll not only allow my weaknesses to be seen; I'll expose myself to potentially being made weaker. Vulnerability, man. I'm not so great at that.

Today's scripture talks about people as jars of clay, which are breakable and therefore vulnerable. They're also not much to look at. They're just vessels for beautiful things to grow in. You don't look at a clay pot and think, *Wow! So sturdy! Wow! So precious! Wow! So special!* No, they're sweet and simple, and they sell them for two dollars at the local hardware store because they're easy to break. They're woundable.

Transparency is good and beautiful; vulnerability is reserved for select individuals who can be trusted to take care of our fragile and simple selves. If we're not sure who we can be vulnerable with, I've got one really beautiful place I think we should start: our Father. Who can be trusted. Who is careful. Who may allow hardship and pain to enter our life for a purpose but is worthy of making us woundable at all times.

Let's take vulnerability too far in the right places, and if we're not sure what those places are, let's start in the throne room of grace. Let's go vulnerable, not just be transparent.

Take Vulnerability Too Far

Be honest about how you think about yourself before God. Do you imagine yourself as a clay pot or a really special ornamental piece of art that needs to be dressed up and cleaned up to be accepted? What would it look like to be truly vulnerable with God?

16 REDEMPTION

Israel, put your hope in the LORD, for with the LORD is unfailing love and with him is full redemption.—PSALM 130:7

It's always going to be this way.

He's always going to be this way.

She's always going to be this way.

This is just the way it is.

That's the way it works.

This is the way things go.

This world, which is wasting away and tasting failure around every corner, will tell us that it's always going to be this way and that change is potentially possible but probably out of our reach. This world, which can only see in flesh and blood, under the constraints of sin and brokenness, will tell us that when it looks like it's over—it probably is. Best to adjust, best to accept, best to anticipate death and defeat and get used to pain because it's always going to be this way.

But God. In His goodness, in His glory, He has always had one path for the humans that He loves so very much, and it's a path of redemption.

But God. In His power, for His pleasure, and for our good, He has a revolving door of redemption where He is continually making things new, making things restored, making things better than we could ask or imagine.

But God. He is kind and redemptive. Full of restoration, always on the move, and always able to bring everything and everyone back from the dead.

This is what He does, this is who He is, and maybe one of the most extreme and wonderful things we can do is simply agree that restoration is what He does and redemption is who He is.

Today let's take it too far and change our language. Let's speak possibility and promise and redemption over ourselves, over our people, and over this world.

Take Redemption Too Far
Instead of saying it's always going to be this way,
what can you speak redemption into today? What or
who can you believe God is not done with yet?

17 TENDERNESS

"And now, here's what I'm going to do: I'm going to start all over again. I'm taking her back out into the wilderness where we had our first date, and I'll court her. I'll give her bouquets of roses. I'll turn Heartbreak Valley into Acres of Hope."—Hosea 2:14 MSG

"Jess is hard on stuff."

My friend was describing me, specifically as it related to my worn-down jacket that I'd just tossed on the floor. I was eighteen and in my freshman college dorm. As the frayed outer garment hit the ground, the words hit my heart. And I haven't forgotten that phrase, said so casually and innocently, for almost two decades.

Jess is hard on stuff.

It's true; I can be. I can love people into exhaustion. I can belabor a point like no one you've ever met. I take it too far! It's what I do. To jackets, foods, people, ideas, and thoughts. I hold on to them tight and squeeze all the goodness out of them, because when I love something, or even like it, I just want more of it.

It's only by the power of the Holy Spirit and many years of failure that I've learned you can love something so much that you take tenderness too far in all the best ways. You can love something the way God does and express it through patience and gentleness; you can love tenderly and expectantly, and that's not weak or holding back.

There's a connection with our Father that takes place when we move toward things, people, ideas, dreams, visions, gifts, and scenarios that we love, while also realizing what kind of love and care that thing, person, idea, or scenario needs.

And sometimes things need tenderness. Sometimes they need tenderness taken too far. Sometimes I need tenderness taken too far. And God always delivers and always teaches me through His intentional care for me.

I can be hard on stuff, but I can also be tender, because I'm made in His image. And being tender can be taking it too far. I can be my fully awake, alive, extreme self and still be tender. Because He is too.

Take Tenderness Too Far

How has God been tender with you? Is there a person, idea, or place that needs some tenderness from you right now? What would it look like to take it too far?

18 HEALTH

> For physical training is of some value, but godliness
> has value for all things, holding promise for both the
> present life and the life to come.—1 TIMOTHY 4:8

Do you have a mentor? A human hero whom you'd love to pattern your life after? Robbi has been one of mine for years. And before Robbi was one of my human heroes, he was my husband's. Robbi is the youth pastor who led us when we met in high school, he was our pastor when we started dating, he is the pastor who married us, and he's the guy I'd call in any crisis. He's just super . . . healthy.

Once, when I was in high school, I saw Robbi walking into the local gym, and I was like, "Oh! You work out? Awesome, Robbi!" And he replied, "I'm just trying to be faithful. I want this body to be healthy for as long as God wants to use it."

Now, twenty years later, I see so much of Robbi in my husband, as Nick is the healthiest person I know. But it doesn't look like you might expect. He doesn't do extreme diets. He doesn't run marathons or do CrossFit for hours on end. He just shows up dutifully to the gym to move and get stronger, and he's intentional about what he puts in his body so he can serve God.

One day we were walking into the gym together as I commented on how strong he was looking lately, and he said, "I'm just trying to be faithful." He smiled and plowed gently ahead while I had major Robbi flashbacks.

In the twenty-first century, the world tells us to take health too far; we've got to be extreme—but honestly, we know better. Extreme spurts of energy and attempts at health are fun, but they don't make us more faithful. They don't necessarily make us healthier overall, but they often take us away from just showing up every day and doing the healthy, simple, fruitful things.

If we want to be healthy, if we want to take health too far, we might just have to keep showing up and being faithful. It might not change the world in a day or have extreme, immediate results, but faithful and healthy decisions compounded over decades, over generations, and aided by the power of God—that changes the world. Let's take it too far.

Take Health Too Far
What's the simplest and healthiest thing you can do today? Take it too far just by being obedient and joyful and expectant. And then try again tomorrow.

19 TENACIOUS

> Then the man said, "Let me go, for it is daybreak." But Jacob replied, "I will not let you go unless you bless me." The man asked him, "What is your name?" "Jacob," he answered. Then the man said, "Your name will no longer be Jacob, but Israel, because you have struggled with God and with humans and have overcome."—Genesis 32:26–28

The story of Jacob, the man who wrestled with God and lived to tell about it, has got to be one of the most interesting in the Bible.

"I will not let you go unless you bless me." He was tenacious.

I heard recently about a revival breaking out on a college campus. People were sharing about it online, this miraculous and beautiful move of God that was taking place. It sounded so incredible! They were seeing people healed, set free, repenting, and finding grace and refreshment. I also heard that this revival movement was preceded by a twentysomething-day prayer gathering. Twenty-plus days of hundreds of people showing up and asking to see God's glory on display. Absolutely a beautiful move of God and by the power of His hand, but it got me thinking . . .

How often do we assume that God is doing something special and otherworldly when really He might just be responding to the tenacity of His kids? I'm asking, Is God moving in special and beautiful ways on this college campus because He loves those students more or because He wants to play favorites? Or is it because they tenaciously and boldly went to the throne room of God for twenty-plus days on end, and when you do that, you can't *help* but see God move?

Which also got me thinking: Is what we call tenacious and bold when it comes to interacting with God really just being obedient and open to who He's said He is and what He's said He'll do?

Was it tenacious of Jacob to wrestle with God and ask for a blessing, or was it just downright prudent given how much God has promised His people? Was it all that wild, or was it just a real, genuine interaction, where someone acknowledged how loving, powerful, and good God can be and asked to see it?

Either way, I wonder what would happen if we took God at His Word. Maybe the world will call it tenacious and we just need to call it belief. I wonder what would happen if we banked on the ability to see His goodness, His glory, and His power displayed in our lives.

Take Tenacity Too Far
Take God at His Word in just one area.
Take one promise He's made you and act
like you believe He'll show up.

20 KINDNESS

Do the riches of his extraordinary kindness make you take him for granted and despise him? Haven't you experienced how kind and understanding he has been to you? Don't mistake his tolerance for acceptance. Do you realize that all the wealth of his extravagant kindness is meant to melt your heart and lead you into repentance?—Romans 2:4 TPT

I once heard Romans 2:4 treated in an almost silly way, definitely taken too far, and it still makes me giggle. A friend of mine was new to the gospel, just figuring out all the workings of sin, righteousness, and the mercy of God, when one of her kids did something disobedient. Instead of disciplining him, she allowed her kid to spank *her*, as she enacted the part of Jesus—being merciful and taking the punishment for her kid.

I'll never forget her sweet, earnest face, telling me about this attempt at gospel-parenting in all seriousness, as I smiled so hard at her compassionate attempt to parent. Now whenever I hear people talk about the kindness of God, I remember her face that day, so wanting to identify with the kindness and mercy of God.

It's His kindness that leads to repentance; there's no getting around it. It's His grace and His goodness that compel us to change, lead us to growth, and change the world for those of us who believe in Him.

But man, we're on the wrong track if we take His kindness to be soft or passive or inactive. Rather, it's an intentional kindness designed to woo our hearts back to His. It's an extraordinary kindness that shows us His character and keeps us remembering that we don't get what we deserve. When we should be far from Him, we're brought close.

Likewise, to agree with God's kindness in our own lives, we don't have to be passive. We don't have to be weak, and I don't think we have to let our kids discipline us. But we can submit ourselves to His love and mercy that are extended to us and extend them to others with the same hopes that they will lead them to see His goodness and worth.

God's kindness is not only about the humans He's serving; it's about His glory and His character being displayed. In the same way, as we're loving and living in the power of His name, we should take kindness too far—for His glory, for His fame, and for others to be compelled by His grace.

Take Kindness Too Far

Be actively kind today. Not just sweet; not fake kind.
Ask God how you can show His kindness to those
you'll come in contact with. You've got this.

21 PRAISE

O my soul, bless God. From head to toe, I'll bless his holy name! O my soul, bless God, don't forget a single blessing!—Psalm 103:1–2 msg

I love that in the Psalms, David often tells his heart what to do.

Praise, soul! Bless God! Sing! Don't forget the good stuff!

The most natural and human inclination of our souls is not always to praise, is it? When I think about the kind of gal I want to be, I know I want to be one who takes praise too far. I want to be the woman who trusts and blesses God in the midst of a hard day. I want to be the kind of woman who gives Him credit when something goes great. But so often my very first reaction is just not praise.

We often have to tell our souls what to do when it comes to God. We have to remind ourselves that praise is what we're meant for; it's our ticket to feeling most at home on this earth because our souls are longing for heaven. We have to remember that it's not about what we feel in the moment, but what we know in light of eternity—that ultimately, worshiping God for the rest of time is what we were made to do. Sometimes we've got to tell our souls to praise.

You can take it too far however you want when it comes to praise, but I think one of the most poignant things we can decide to do as children

41

of God living on earth is just intentionally starting the praise. Use your words. Use your prayers. Turn on some music and sing to the One who created music and joy. Go for a walk and appreciate what God has created. Tell Him out loud how thankful you are for your surroundings. Whatever you do—just start.

Praising God and thinking about praising God—they're different. And they have different outcomes. Praising God and wanting to be the kind of gal who praises God—different, different outcomes. If praising Him is what we're made for, what connects us to Him, no matter how we do it, it just matters that we actually start.

Take Praise Too Far
Praise God today. By yourself or with a group, for ten minutes or two hours. Bless the Lord, O your soul. Take it too far.

22 PURPOSE

I know that you can do all things; no purpose
of yours can be thwarted.—Job 42:2

If I were the enemy, and I couldn't actually thwart God's plans for anyone's life, I'd use fear, comparison, and insecurity as tools to keep God's people from experiencing abundance. When I think about the really beautiful days of my life that have been shaded with fear, comparison, and insecurity, I'm sick and tired and done. There I was, ready to be used by God, ready to see and seek His purpose for my life, having everything I needed because He'd given it to me . . . but I became riddled with doubt.

I'm ready to experience my days as God made me to: full of love and expectancy, not fear. Declaring the ground He's given me blessed and good, not looking to the left or the right in anxious comparison. I'm ready to spend my days believing in God's capacity in my life instead of partnering with feelings of insecurity and inadequacy—as if it were my power that accomplished anything. I'm ready to stop doubting God's good purpose and how He plans to bring it to fruition.

If I were the enemy, I'd use fear and comparison and insecurity to keep me from seeing that *these are days of abundance*. But too bad, bro. We know Truth, and He is telling a different story. These *are* the days. This is a God dream. Abundance is here, on earth as it is in heaven.

In today's scripture, Job makes a bold and beautiful statement about God's purpose after a painful period, and we're told that God accepted his prayer and then blessed his face off.

May we be able to say, on the best and most beautiful days, "I trust God's purpose for my life, and I won't miss out on the abundance that's right here." But also, on the horrible and painful days, may we also trust His plan with everything we have, not looking to the left or the right, but firmly holding on for all that He's got for us.

Take Purpose Too Far

Write a purpose statement for today. What do you
have on your plate, and how do you think God
is going to show up in and through you?

23 SUBMISSION

> Submit yourselves for the Lord's sake to every human authority:
> whether to the emperor, as the supreme authority, or to
> governors, who are sent by him to punish those who do wrong
> and to commend those who do right.—1 Peter 2:13–14

Don't get nervous; we're not going to stay on the subject of submission long. I have heard some really harmful talk and teaching about submission in my day. I've heard disastrous and painful things about what it means to submit in marriage, submit to religious authority, and some advice that's just made me flat out laugh. Once I heard a Bible teacher say that submission in marriage is just learning to duck so God hits your husband and not you. I don't think that's theologically correct, but it is funny to laugh at.

We've probably all heard some flawed teaching about submission, but let's not throw the baby out with the bathwater. In fact, if we reject the entire idea of submission, Satan wins and we miss out. Because the idea of being submitted to authority and leadership in a healthy way is an idea that grows our humility and our understanding and increases order in our lives.

We see submission among the Trinity, the triune Godhead—the Son submitting to the Father and creating anticipation for the Spirit. Submission can be beautiful.

45

The question really comes down to this: Are we willing to be led? Are we willing to be led by God? By our bosses? By those He's placed in leadership over us? If they're human, we have to remember that they're fallible and need Jesus like we do. They aren't any more loved by Him or equipped by Him, but He places people in leadership roles so we can function and get stuff done and move forward without looking around and trying to figure out who is in charge.

To take submission too far, I vote we find Christlike people who lead in a servant-hearted way and let God lead us through them. We don't need to make them our gods or the prime authority in our lives, but we can learn and move and grow beneath their care.

Let's take submission to God too far by letting Him do what He wants in our life, grow what He wants in our life, take us where He wants to go in our life. Let's trust His power and presence to do the heavy lifting, and let's let Him be in charge.

Take Submission Too Far

Is there any part of your life you've not submitted to God? Is there an area in which you hesitate to give Him power or authority? Give it back to Him with an action today. You know what to do. Take it too far!

24 ACCESS

The news about him spread all the more, so that crowds of people came to hear him and to be healed of their sicknesses. But Jesus often withdrew to lonely places and prayed.—Luke 5:15–16

I'm not sure how it worked when Jesus was on earth. He was fully human and fully God, so we can only guess about what His access to His Father was like. In my head, I want to believe that they had some kind of walkie-talkie system worked out, where they could just talk back and forth. But my theology tells me that's a human interpretation, and they're much more closely linked than that. One God, three incarnations. They share the same heart, the same mind, the same will.

What we do know is that Jesus took His access and availability to God seriously, and we've got recorded proof of His prayer time—both private and public. Hebrews 4:16 says to walk boldly to the throne of grace (NKJV). Jesus took the opportunities He had to go and talk to the Father. He took His access to heaven seriously, and so can we.

In Luke 11:1 we're told that the disciples asked Jesus how to pray, which proves to me that sometimes when you're talking to God, you feel like you're doing it wrong. They were *talking to God*, asking God *how to talk to God*. That's pretty cute and sweet and humble, if you ask me.

47

But we should learn from them and appreciate the access we've been given. Even if we feel intimidated by the idea of talking to the God who made the universe, we get to do it, and that should be enough to get us in the space of being grateful to utilize our access to Him.

Jesus took His earthly access and ability to commune with the Father seriously, so let's follow in His footsteps. Let's not get tripped up about the how and the method; let's just talk to God. Let's take it too far by actually stepping into the eternal conversation that He started when He called us individually by our names.

Take Access Too Far

Spend five minutes talking to God today. Go on a walk or sit in your car or journal your words. The only rule is they have to be real; don't say what you think you should say. Just talk to your Father.

25 BELIEF

[The Samaritans] said to the woman, "We no longer believe just because of what you said; now we have heard for ourselves, and we know that this man really is the Savior of the world."—John 4:42

This passage took place right after Jesus had His beautiful interaction with the Samaritan woman at the well. He combated sexism and racism and shame in one fell swoop and extended new life, hope, freedom, and meaning into her life just before she ran off to share the good news with others. She rushed into town and told her story about what He had said to her, and the people of her village came to meet Him for themselves. Then they declared that they were ready to believe because of the word that He'd spoken into them.

The word *belief* that's used here is *pisteuó*, and it means what you'd imagine: to believe, have faith in, entrust with. What I want to capture here is this: so many people think that they're supposed to blindly believe in Jesus, based on the word of other humans, without anything else to assure them about who He is or what He does. But here's the thing: Jesus is consistently faithful to move, speak, and heal individual people over and over and over again.

You don't have to take other people's words about Jesus and build a faith around them. You can go straight to Him, let Him speak to you, and then place your trust in Him based on your specific interaction with Him. He's big enough and good enough to faithfully enable that.

The testimony of others may spark our interest; it may spur our faith; it may impart courage and speak life over our belief—but we can go to Jesus and get all we need to truly trust. We can go to Him and hear what *He* has to say.

Take Belief Too Far
Take it too far and ask God to build your belief today.

26 CHARITY

"Each and every day he will supply your needs as you seek his kingdom passionately, above all else. So don't ever be afraid, dearest friends! Your loving Father joyously gives you his kingdom realm with all its promises! So, now, go and sell what you have and give to those in need, making deposits in your account in heaven, an account that will never be taken from you. Your gifts will become a secure and unfailing treasure, deposited in heaven forever."—LUKE 12:31–33 TPT

If this devotional were called *Keep It Lukewarm*, we could have a whole entry about charity and how we don't have to take it too far. We could list all the reasons Luke 12:31–33 is too strongly worded a passage, and we could find ways to exclude ourselves from its truth. We could do that, except the book is called *Take It Too Far*—so let's stick with that theme.

In today's passage, this is Jesus talking, and He's speaking pretty plainly: Don't be scared. Your Father will meet your needs. Go and sell what you've got and help out those who need it. It's not your bank account that matters, but what you deposit into heaven.

He takes it too far; there's not really anything we need to do to enhance that, to pour gas on the flames.

So it seems like the best way we can approach this passage is to pause here and ask, What keeps us from being obedient in this area? Is it fear? Is it selfishness? Is it pride? Is it our culture?

When did we stop taking Jesus' teaching to heart and start calling it extreme, when we agree with all the premises surrounding it? We agree that He'll meet our needs; we agree that it's good to serve others. We agree that it's what we build eternally and not in our accounts that matters. So what would it look like to combine all those truths, trust His Word, and live this out?

Take Charity Too Far

Is there anything you can sell on Craigslist or Facebook Marketplace today to give that money away? It doesn't have to be huge, but it would be cool to literally agree with this wisdom Jesus imparted to us today.

27 DISCIPLINE

> "The people I love, I call to account—prod and correct and guide so that they'll live at their best. Up on your feet, then! About face! Run after God!"—REVELATION 3:19 MSG

If I didn't love my kids and didn't want good for them, I would totally let them be horrible brats. If I didn't love them and I didn't care about their futures, I'd give them candy and ice cream all day, and I wouldn't ever tell them when they made a huge misstep.

Instead, because I love them and want good for them, I tell them not to eat too many sweets. Because I love them and want good for them, I gently let them know when they're being a bad friend. Because I love them and want good for them, I teach them how to be respectful humans—which often means correcting them. Because I love them, I discipline them.

It is because God loves us that He points out our sin, corrects us in grace and patience, and disciplines us in His love. It is because He loves us that He guides us in His kindness to repent, to be refreshed by starting over again. And it's always good for us because we're shifted; we're changed; we're grown for the better.

Sometimes God corrects us through other people; sometimes He does it via His Word, sometimes by the power of the Spirit. But no matter how He does it, may we be people who humbly and hopefully take His discipline with open hands, knowing He loves us, wants good for us, and is making us into image bearers who give Him glory and change the world.

Take Discipline Too Far

Is there a moment in the recent past where you felt
God's discipline? Can you thank Him for it today,
count the fruits it grew in you, and tell someone
else how it changed you for the better?

28 UNITY

I urge you, my brothers and sisters, for the sake of the name of
our Lord Jesus Christ, to agree to live in unity with one another
and put to rest any division that attempts to tear you apart. Be
restored as one united body living in perfect harmony. Form a
consistent choreography among yourselves, having a common
perspective with shared values.—1 Corinthians 1:10 TPT

I don't think anyone *wants* disunity. I don't think any soul wakes
up wanting to be in conflict with other humans, much less other
Christians. But sometimes we get there quickly; other times it's because
of years and years of small shifts, pain, or moments of pride. But once
we're there, it's hard to get back to a place of peace. "Hard" is often
an understatement; sometimes conflict and disunity seem downright
insurmountable.

Here's what I capture from this passage about how we can take unity
too far, how we can go after it with our eyes on God's glory: it takes
supernatural help from God, and it takes intentional steps on our part as
well. We have to pray and ask God to do what only He can do, but we've
got to use our hands, our hearts, our words, and our humility to do what
we can do to promote unity.

55

God will bring supernatural help; the Spirit will do the heavy lifting, but let's show up with a desire to use what we've got in ways that we can.

Take Unity Too Far

Where is there disunity in your life right now? Have you asked God for help? Do you believe that this is not beyond His reach? What can you do using your words, your hands, and your God-given humility to help today?

29 FORGIVENESS

Be kind and compassionate to one another, forgiving each
other, just as in Christ God forgave you.—Ephesians 4:32

I was in high school when this boy Seth made fun of my dress. It was a shirtdress; it looked like a collared shirt that was extended. I walked into church, feeling fly in my shirtdress, when Seth wrinkled his nose and said, "Nice . . . uh . . . shirt? Dress? Which is it? It's like it couldn't make its mind up." That was almost twenty years ago. And I still remember it.

Holding bitterness and unforgiveness in our hearts, man! It's a doozy! That hurt was about a silly comment, but most of us are walking around with real pain, real wrongs that have been done to us, and real people who are incredibly hard to forgive. We've been taken advantage of, we've been hurt accidentally, and some of us have had wrongs committed against us that were very intentional and malicious.

How in the world are we supposed to forgive?

About a year ago, a friend hurt me a lot, and at the time, I was seeing a Christian counselor who was helping me process the pain. I kept a note on my phone of questions, feelings, and confusing thoughts I had regarding this situation. It was complicated, lots of people were involved, and I needed help sorting out my thoughts so I didn't act out of my pain.

One question I kept at the top of the notes in my phone was: *How do I forgive and not get bitter?*

I was in a worship service a few months later, thinking about the sin I'd been pardoned for. I thought about how much Jesus loved me in spite of my own junk, then I pulled out my phone and typed in the only answer I knew that would satisfy my soul.

How do I forgive and not get bitter? The cross.

No matter how much we've been hurt, the cross of Christ, the sacrifice our perfect Savior made for our sin, that's the answer to how we forgive and move forward without bitterness. Because He was able to, we are able to.

The friend who hurt me is no longer my friend. That relationship wasn't healthy for us. But when I think about her, I smile. I want God's best for her. And it's only because of the cross that I'm able to do that.

Taking forgiveness too far doesn't mean we turn a blind eye to pain or keep unhealthy people in our lives. It just means we remember how much we've been pardoned and allow that same grace to be offered for others, not just for us.

Take Forgiveness Too Far

Today, just start by making a list of people you need to forgive. Write their names down and ask Jesus to help. That's a huge start. That's taking it too far.

30 PASSION

When the hour came, Jesus and his apostles reclined at the table. And he said to them, "I have eagerly desired to eat this Passover with you before I suffer."—Luke 22:14–15

Every single devotion in this book could be summed up with this sentence: whatever you're doing, do it with passion. Take it too far, right? The Greek word for passion that's found most often in the New Testament is *epithumia*, and it means "longing, desire, passion." Most often in Scripture, it's used to describe ungodly passions that we need to quit or hand to Jesus so we can live holy lives.

So if we don't really dig, we could only assume that passion has to do with unhealthy rhythms, actions, or activities that don't bring God glory and don't agree with what He's written over our lives.

But here's why I love looking a little deeper at the Greek: we find that the same word is often interpreted in different ways, and we'd totally miss it if we didn't slow down to check. The word *epithumia* that means "passion, desire, longing"—it's the same one Jesus used right before His death when He described His stance toward eating with His disciples. And not just any old meal, but the one that we would carry on for thousands of years to remember and celebrate the fact that He's given His body and His blood that we might be united with God and redeemed by His sacrifice.

He is passionate about us. He is passionate about redemption. He is passionate about salvation and resurrection and His rescue plan for our lives. Make no mistake: passion is not an invention of the world that we need to cut out of our lives. We can be passionate in all the good, holy, beautiful activities of heaven because we are made in the image of God, and He is passionate.

If we're looking for a quiet or passive God to follow, we're going to be disappointed. God was so passionate about His relationship with you that He gave up His Son. Jesus was so passionate about you taking your place in the kingdom that He went to the cross for you specifically and for us as a whole. The Spirit is so passionate about being your Helper and Comforter that He intercedes for you constantly—bringing you peace and communion and even more passion, because passion is from God.

Take Passion Too Far
Ask God to give you a heart and a mind that don't want to hold back. Ask Him to help you see His passion and mirror it in your own life.

31 SELF-CONTROL

For the Spirit God gave us does not make us timid, but gives us power, love and self-discipline.—2 Timothy 1:7

Here's something interesting to me: in this pretty well-known passage, timidity, or fear, is pitted against power, love, and self-discipline. I get the power. If you're walking in timidity and fear, you're probably not accessing God's power or believing in His power at work in and through you. And I get love, because both Scripture and science tell us that love and fear are opposite emotions. So I understand that it's important that we know we're not made in the image of fear; we're not made to live that out but rather to speak and show the love of God with all we've got.

But self-discipline is an interesting one. It kind of makes you pause. Do fear and timidity keep us from acting out of self-discipline or self-control? I don't automatically think of those two as opposites. Until, that is, I remember every time I've ever tried to start a healthy habit or begin a new rhythm that seems wise for my life.

I'm scared it's going to cost me. I'm scared of what I'll lose out on or miss out on if I continually exhibit this healthy behavior. What if I can't keep going? What if it turns out I'm actually just lazy and bad at the thing I know I'm supposed to do?

Sometimes I'm scared to exhibit self-discipline because I'm nervous I'll be too good at something. What if I stick to this habit or press into this plan God has given me and I'm successful and blessed and that changes my life? For some of us, the change that would accompany success is actually more terrifying than sticking with the status quo. What if I'm rejected? What if I lose my comfort? What if it's hard? What if it's not?

Okay, actually . . . I totally understand how fear and self-discipline are pitted against each other. So how do we take self-control too far? We fight the fear and remember that we were made in the image of God and given power, love, and self-discipline so that we could not only be obedient but experience His abundance. We take it too far and take the next step and agree with who God has made us to be.

Take Self-Control Too Far

What act of self-discipline would you do today if you knew
you didn't have to be scared? What would you do if you weren't
afraid of failure because the grace of God holds you?

32 SELFLESSNESS

> "Give, and it will be given to you. Good measure, pressed down, shaken together, running over, will be put into your lap. For with the measure you use it will be measured back to you."—Luke 6:38 ESV

You've heard the helpful phrase, right? "Humility isn't thinking less of yourself; it's about thinking of yourself less." I love that one. It helps me understand something about humility, and it makes me curious about self-less-ness. I have to say it like that: self-less-ness, really slow, to gather my thoughts and center myself on this idea of not centering on myself.

But I have a thought about selflessness that I hope encourages you. If nothing else, it might surprise you. I don't really think we can do anything that is purely selfless. It's not because I think we're super selfish and we only want good for ourselves. That is the case a lot of the time, but we have access to humility and the character of Christ, so we can do things that are actually focused on the good of others.

I just don't know that we can ever do anything truly selfless and not be blessed in return. Ultimately, when we center on others, their good, and God's glory, we *win* because we experience more of Him. We see Him more clearly, we are able to identify with Him and who He's made us to be, and we see humans we love grow and change and get good stuff, and that feels good to us.

I recited this Luke 6 passage a lot during my first pregnancy. I just hoped, hoped, hoped that the sacrifice I was about to make would come back to me at some point. I hoped, hoped, hoped that the sleeplessness and the heartburn and the financial burden would be shaken together, pressed down, and would come out running over.

But what I couldn't prepare for was the lifetime of extreme blessing that came just from loving my son. In an attempt to do something selfless, I was blessed nonetheless, because that is the economy of the kingdom. That's how it works when we walk with God.

Take selflessness too far. Really perceive what is good for others, and go after it with all you've got. But don't expect to sit there poor and lonely and unhappy after you do. You'll win the same way God won His glory when He sent His Son to the cross for our sins. In the kingdom, when you give—you get. And there's just no getting around it.

Take Selflessness Too Far

Pick one person and ask God what you could do for him or her that would be selfless. Then remember to count the fruit when He blesses and grows you through the experience.

33 UNDERSTANDING

The beginning of wisdom is this: Get wisdom. Though it
cost all you have, get understanding.—Proverbs 4:7

Recently some friends of ours were embroiled in conflict with another
group of people, and we were burdened for them. It was a sad situation—a
bunch of people who know and love God and want others to know and
love God, yet they were at an impasse and couldn't get on the same page.

I could sit and listen to either group of people talk about where they
were coming from, and I could hear why they'd gotten upset, what felt
real to them, and what they thought the solution could be. Both sides
seemed reasonable, yet they were so far apart. I started to think, *This is
it. This incredibly difficult-to-handle process of understanding others is what
changes the world and sets it on fire sometimes. We have wisdom, we have
knowledge, but we don't always have understanding.*

It's so hard to put down your own thoughts, feelings, and needs for
long enough to hear someone else's. It takes real Spirit-empowered work
not only to listen but to want to understand enough to see conflict come
to an end and peace prevail. Wisdom is helpful, knowledge gives you
insight, but if you want to change the world, try to understand how someone else got where they are and where they're coming from.

The good news is this: we *can* do this because Christ did it for us. We *can* access understanding because we have a Savior who made us in His image, then came to earth in compassion and grace to show us *how* to access understanding. It may take some pausing. It may take trying over and over again, but we are able to take understanding too far and know that on the other side of it, there is always grace and mercy—the same that we've been given.

Take Understanding Too Far

Today, take time to hear someone else's story. Ask them questions, not in accusation but with an intent to understand. Ask God to give you eyes and ears to see and hear them the way He does.

34 WISDOM

> But the wisdom that comes from heaven is first of all pure;
> then peace-loving, considerate, submissive, full of mercy
> and good fruit, impartial and sincere.—JAMES 3:17

Have you ever met someone who is supersmart but not super kind? I'm sad to say I absolutely have. I'm also sad to say that while I'm not worldly-wise in many areas, there have been times when I've gained insight or knowledge in a certain area and lorded it over others with pride. In the moment, it made me feel good. It made me feel like I belonged, but when I look back on those moments, I realize that my momentary feelings of worth were never justified by the discouragement I brought to others.

God showed me an idea a few years ago that has helped me keep my hands open when it comes to the knowledge that He brings. He showed me that having knowledge and wisdom is a privilege, and I have them, like every other good gift in my life, only because He allowed me to have them at that moment. So to act with pride and disdain for anyone who doesn't currently have them doesn't make sense. I know what I know only because He's shown me what He's shown me.

I don't want to feel shame for what I don't know yet, so I certainly don't want anyone else to feel shame about what *they* don't know yet.

Wisdom, knowing something, is helpful only if it's coupled with all the other good attributes of being a Jesus follower. Wisdom plus mercy changes the world. Wisdom plus consideration of others' feelings shifts everything. Wisdom plus purity and sincerity—we would want to make the person with *that* combination of qualities our foremost politician, right?

Just knowing stuff to know stuff doesn't do anything but puff us up. Wisdom that leads to godly change and repentance and healing and help—that changes everything. Let's go after wisdom, let's take it too far, and let's do it with the grace and gentleness that Jesus embodies for us.

Take Wisdom Too Far

How can you use the wisdom He's given
you today in a way that also embodies
compassion, mercy, and sincerity?

35 INTEGRITY

Finally, brothers and sisters, whatever is true, whatever is noble, whatever is right, whatever is pure, whatever is lovely, whatever is admirable—if anything is excellent or praiseworthy—think about such things.—Philippians 4:8

They say that all emotions are rooted either in fear or love. Here's what I find when it comes to talking about integrity: I get very, very fearful. How can I do everything right? How can I know the right things to do? What if I make a misstep? What if someone catches me being human and my integrity is questioned? What if we're all just really busted humans, and none of us have any integrity? Any of these questions ever roll around in your mind?

Have you heard of the TV show *The Good Place*? It's a hilarious and interesting comedy series about what happens when we die, and it features a group of individuals who start questioning and looking into the process of living for eternity. After a few seasons they summarize this beautiful bad news of the gospel: it's too hard to be a human. Even when you want to do good, you do bad, and doing bad is utterly inevitable.

If TV shows that are not about God are pointing to this inevitable fear that we all carry, I'd say it's worth asking the question, What happens when we just can't be people of integrity all the time?

The good news is this: *what* happens is Jesus. He makes a way. He brings the grace and the righteousness and the help, because He stood in our place, taking the death and the shame that we deserve so we could experience the resurrection He purchased.

But now what? What do we do now that He's stood in the gap for us? How do we run after integrity now that our standing with God is secured?

Enter Philippians 4:8, and we can all take a deep breath: What's true? What's noble? What's right, pure, and lovely? What would you want to be doing if God were watching you . . . which He is? Do those things; think about those things; run after those things. Feel the grace when you make a mistake, and step back into the light. It's not your integrity that brings you close to God, but the perfection and righteousness of Jesus, so rest assured. You just get to think on the good things to experience more of Him on earth.

This really is good news.

Take Integrity Too Far

Is there anything you're spending your time thinking about
or doing that you know is not pure, lovely, true, or noble?
Can you stop today? Confess and ask God for help.

36 RIGHTEOUSNESS

God made him who had no sin to be sin for us, so that in him we might become the righteousness of God.—2 Corinthians 5:21

There are certain words that really need context to help us know how we feel about them. Case in point: *bear.*

"I bought my son a teddy bear today." That's cute! That's sweet!

"The hiker got mauled by a vicious black bear today." That's awful! How tragic! Why, God?!

One of those words from the Bible that can easily get me tripped up without context is *righteousness.* Before I became a believer, the only kind of righteousness I heard about—self-righteousness—sounded awful.

Here's how the dictionary defines *self-righteous*: "confident of one's own righteousness, especially when smugly moralistic and intolerant of the opinions and behavior of others."[1]

Um, that sounds awful. That also sounds like how a lot of the world describes Christians, which should break our hearts and cause us to pause.

Righteousness is defined as "acting in accord with divine or moral law, free from guilt or sin."[2] And we know that attribute can be applied to us only by the power of God, propelled by the love of God and the saving work of Jesus on the cross.

Jesus became sin so that we might become righteous. And how do we stay righteous? By doing everything good for the rest of our lives? No, just by being a part of the family of God—His reputation covers ours. When God looks at us, He sees His Son.

Believing in and talking about the righteousness that comes from God, even agreeing with what He's written over our lives with our actions—that is beautiful.

Using our God-given, Jesus-purchased righteousness as a weapon to hurt others? Not beautiful, not good, and not the way we want to take it too far.

If being *self*-righteous means being confident of how good we are, smug toward others we deem as not good, and unopen to the experiences of others, then may we take it too far with the *God-given* righteousness that we possess.

Take Righteousness Too Far
Tell God how good He is today, and ask Him to
help you be hopeful about how His righteousness
can transform anyone, even you.

37 FOCUS

Every believer was faithfully devoted to following the teachings of the apostles. Their hearts were mutually linked to one another, sharing communion and coming together regularly for prayer.—ACTS 2:42 TPT

There's a big obsession right now in our culture regarding balance. How do we balance everything? We all want to know how we keep and maintain balance so that everything feels equal and fair and right and normal. I've got a beef with balance, and I'd like to introduce an alternative way, which I believe is not necessarily imbalance, but focus. Here's why:

1. Balance denotes that somehow if we stack everything just so, we can have all the things in our stack. We can be good or great at everything and have Pinterest-worthy homes. To be honest, I just don't know that we can or that we should. We're limited. We're finite. We have only so many hours in a day. We may have to pick and choose what feels most important to us.

2. Balance speaks to a normalizing, and I just want to know: Who is picking what is normal for me? Who is saying what is normal? Is it culture? Is it the church? Is it magazines? If we're all striving for balance, who is deciding when it's all good and equal?

You won't find a lot in Scripture about balance. In fact, Jesus said a lot of *wild* things that, if followed, mean we'll live really imbalanced lives. Sell everything and give it to the poor? Not balanced. Take up your cross and follow Me? Not balanced.

I love today's passage from Acts 2, the genesis of the church as we know it. I want you to know that nothing about their lives was normal. They were going to church *every day*; some of us struggle to make it three times a month. They were devoted to being taught; they were committed to one another, and that probably did not look so balanced and normal in comparison to the rest of their culture.

But this is how we were built. A bunch of individuals, impacted by Jesus, and focused on His glory and the good of others. What has He asked you to focus on? Do you think you'll get where He wants to take you by focusing or making sure it fits into the world's picture of . . . balance?

Take Focus Too Far

Is there an area of life you've been holding back in because you want it to seem healthy or acceptable to others? How can you take it too far today?

38 WELCOME

Therefore welcome one another as Christ has welcomed you, for the glory of God.—Romans 15:7 esv

Have you seen the new thing churches are doing with people holding signs out front? We have them at our church, and I love it. Our people hold square signs that are about two and a half by two and a half feet, and they have cute sayings on them. They're nice because they show new visitors where the door is and they also give people greeting something to do with their hands. As an introvert, I appreciate something to do with my hands when I'm saying hello to strangers.

But a lot of churches use the phrase "Welcome Home" on their signs, and when I asked my husband (also my pastor) if our signs could say that, he politely declined. His reasoning: the church, here on earth, isn't our home—heaven is. We want people to feel welcome, but we want them to know this isn't it. This isn't the best part. We're not Jesus, and this is not heaven.

I love that he thinks deeply about stuff like that, but the point remains: *we want to make people feel welcome.* And signs that say, "Welcome to this place that isn't home and isn't heaven but hopefully will be encouraging!" just don't have the same vibes.

So how do we make people feel truly welcome? Thank God for Romans 15:7.

We greet them like Jesus greeted us. Gladly.

We rejoice with them like heaven rejoices for us. Full of celebration.

We love them like the Father loves us. With grace and truth.

We consider them like God considers us. Worthy of our time and attention.

We can welcome people the same way we were welcomed, even if we don't have cute signs or coffee to offer. We can take welcoming too far with exactly what we've been given by God: our hands, our mouths, our attention, our affection.

Take this welcoming too far because you've been welcomed well by God Himself. This is what we get to do.

Take Welcoming Too Far

Greet someone like God would today. See how
it changes your entire interaction.

39 STEADFAST

Therefore, my dear brothers and sisters, stand firm.
Let nothing move you.—1 Corinthians 15:58

Once, a few years ago, our family was in a season of major upheaval and transition. My husband was applying for a job that would mean a big shift for us, and we just were not sure what was next. I was feeling tossed in the wind every few days when we'd get a call or word about what we thought might happen.

In the midst of that time, I went on a run in this park that had huge, tall, skinny trees surrounding the running path. There were hundreds of them, reaching far into the sky and stretching out on the horizon in front of me.

God, I want to be like these trees! I thought. *I want to be planted in one place. I want to have time to grow. I want to be unmovable, but this season of transition has me looking this way and that, unsure of what's next, not able to settle down or sit down or put down roots.*

And then I felt it, that strong wave of conviction and correction from God as I remembered this: your earthly standing and situation has nothing to do with the steadfastness and settled feeling you have access to through God.

Even when life is going *nuts*, so much can seem settled because His love, affection, grace, mercy, and strength are always the same. His power, His presence, His work in and through us—steadfast. They're not going anywhere, and there are no plans for them to change for the rest of eternity.

We can stand firm when the whole world is shaking. We can be rooted when we don't even have time to unpack our bags. We can take faithfulness and steadfastness too far because Christ did the same for us and made us in His image. We can keep our eyes on Him, the author and the finisher—even when nothing seems settled or sure.

It doesn't make any sense, but it's the very good news that is our reality. The trees have nothing on our Father; He made them, you know. The chaos and confusion aren't daunting to Him; He allowed them for our good and His glory.

Take Steadfastness Too Far
Name one way God has been faithful or
steadfast in your life lately. What would it
look like for you to live unshaken today?

40 REPENTANCE

Repent, then, and turn to God, so that your sins may be wiped out, that times of refreshing may come from the Lord, and that he may send the Messiah, who has been appointed for you—even Jesus.—Acts 3:19–20

You know the Bible passages that you'll never forget? Acts 3:19–20 is one of those for me, and while that may seem pretty random to you, it's been formative for me.

I was in my early twenties when a friend and I were helping prep for a women's retreat at our church. The theme of the weekend was refreshment, and the leaders were taking it too far in the best ways. We had spa-themed stuff, we'd planned pedicures for the ladies, and everything was spa colored—light blues and teals and soft fabrics. My friend Kalle was teaching one of the sessions, and I was helping her prepare—by praying for her mostly, but also searching the Word for verses on refreshment.

We came across Acts 3:19–20 and couldn't find anything else so explicit about how to be refreshed. Both Kalle and I felt nervous for her to deliver this message—a young gal in her twenties in a room full of women who have been walking with God much longer than we had? Could she just come in and call everyone to repent?

She did, and it was beautiful. And God marked my heart with this passage for the rest of my life. In fact, I can recite Acts 3:19–20 better than I can John 3:16.

That's because I've consistently found it to be *true*. Nothing brings peace and refreshment to my heart like telling God I'm sorry and asking for His help to turn myself around. *Repentance* has become this big, bad, scary word to us, mostly because of how humans have misused it, and we assume that it means to sit in condemnation or fear, to leach all the enjoyable things out of our lives. Rather, it just means to turn back to God, toward Him—not away—no longer hiding, but holding up our hearts for Him to heal and mend.

The Word is true. This is where the refreshment comes. This is where the hope floods in. This is where the light hits the darkest parts and we take a deep breath again.

We are safe to take repentance too far, to tell the Lord we're sorry, and to see how relief floods in. This is what we were made for.

Take Repentance Too Far
Just acknowledge one area of your life today
where you need to turn back to God. Hold
it up to Him and ask for His help.

41 CALLING

> And Jesus came up and spoke to them, saying, "All authority
> has been given to Me in heaven and on earth. Go therefore and
> make disciples of all the nations, baptizing them in the name
> of the Father and the Son and the Holy Spirit, teaching them
> to observe all that I commanded you; and lo, I am with you
> always, even to the end of the age."—Matthew 28:18–20 NASB

When you're not sure what to do, just do the last thing you were told. That's what I tell my kids: "If you get confused, just go back to the last thing you were sure I told you and work toward that."

The last thing Jesus said as He was ascending into heaven was to go and make disciples. To paraphrase, "Tell everyone about Me, and let them know how great it is that they get to walk with Me."

Does this mean that we all need to quit our jobs and become pastors? Absolutely not. But I do think that it means we can put aside some stress and fretting when it comes to knowing what we're on earth to do. And I also think it means we can press past the fear that comes when we think we're not equipped to tell people about Jesus.

If you're a nanny, you can make disciples. If you're a barista, you can make disciples. If you're a banker or good at singing or a schoolteacher or a nurse or a sanitation worker or a dishwasher, your calling is clear: make disciples.

We take this process of using what we've got—our stories and our struggles and our strengths and our weaknesses—and letting the light of Jesus hit them so that we can fulfill our callings and take it too far. God brings the Word, the power, the authority, and the life change, and we simply show up—needing God and telling others about Him, for His glory and their good.

Take Calling Too Far

Take a moment today to write down where you
think you'll be going and who you think you'll be
interacting with. And then ask God to send you in His
power, His authority, and under the banner of this
calling to take His love and grace and light too far.

42 COMPASSION

Therefore, as God's chosen people, holy and dearly loved, clothe yourselves with compassion, kindness, humility, gentleness and patience. —COLOSSIANS 3:12

My daughter and I are both feelers. We can access, describe, and express our feelings quite easily. You can pray for my husband and our boys right now if you want to, because wow—do they get a lot of emotions expressed toward them on the regular.

But I've noticed over the years, as I watch my little mini-me, that her emotions expressed for others and their pain (not just her own) are often more easily accessed than mine. I first noticed it when we visited New York City and we took her on the subway. I knew that the socially respectable thing to do was (a) not stare at anyone and (b) act as if I don't see what's happening around me; in other words, be aloof. But she didn't have those social cues, and her response was staggering.

She people-watched, viewing the life and beauty and abundance around her, but she also glimpsed the pain—taking it all in. She'd look around, absorbing it all, until her compassionate heart couldn't possibly hold any more—and at that point she'd pull her knees into her chest, tuck her head between them, and close her eyes. She would reach the point of compassion fatigue, feeling so beautifully and deeply for others, and she'd retreat to a healthy place again.

It was in watching her that I realized I had done that on a bigger scale, years ago, except I'd never poked my head back out. After a few intense years of ministry and serving others, I reached a brink where I burned out on feeling the pain of others, so I figuratively tucked my head between my knees and never came back out.

Because of that, I spent a few years seeing and serving others but not letting myself feel for them. I spent time perceiving their pain but not allowing myself to have compassion.

And in the end, I wasn't protecting myself—I was actually just missing out on this beautiful Christlike characteristic that He's given me to power me through life.

We can take compassion too far, opening our eyes and seeing the pain of others, because Jesus never looked away, and He wants us to experience the same abundance.

Take Compassion Too Far

Ask God to help you see just one person today the way
He does. Ask Him to help you love them, perceive their
pain, and feel the hope that He has for their life.

43 PEACE OF MIND

> Finally, be strong in the Lord and in his mighty power. Put
> on the full armor of God, so that you can take your stand
> against the devil's schemes.—EPHESIANS 6:10–11

I have always thought this phrase from Ephesians 6 is so interesting: *"and with your feet fitted with the readiness that comes from the gospel of peace"* (v. 15).

Readiness, *gospel*, and *peace* are all words that sound like they go together, but they do make me pause and think when I'm trying to understand just *how* they go together. This verse is smack-dab in the middle of Ephesians 6, the description of how we get spiritually dressed, and our shoes apparently have something to do with readiness, gospel, and peace.

So let's break down these words and look at the Greek behind them, shall we? First: *readiness*. That word is ἑτοιμασία, which in Greek means "firm footing or preparedness." *Gospel* is a word we're probably familiar with, but one that is always worth revisiting. The Greek for this word is εὐαγγέλιον, and it refers to the good news of the Messiah. And last, our main word, *peace*, is from the Greek word εἰρήνη, which means "quietness, peace of mind, or rest."

When we smash all those together, we get something like this: you are prepared to go anywhere at any time, standing on firm ground because the good news that Jesus came and died for your sins and rose that you might have new life means that you can have peace of mind at all times.

It's not that good worldly outcomes equate to our peace, because we already have the good news. It's not that when we feel like we have everything lined up according to the world's standards, we're ready, because Jesus brings the power and the preparation we often need. It's not that we'll stand on firm ground when our entire life is put together and all the things are figured out—but rather that we're ready at any time to experience peace because of the work Jesus did on the cross.

Peace—walking in it and taking it everywhere we go—isn't so much something we earn or work our way up to as it is a personal choice to agree and believe that God has given us this option to take it too far and walk, run, and move in the peace of mind we've been so freely given.

Take Peace of Mind Too Far

Where are you headed to today? Write one sentence that declares how it changes things to know you're headed there with the good news that Jesus made a way for you, rescued your soul, and gave your life purpose.

44 WONDER

> Everyone was amazed and gave praise to God. They were filled with awe and said, "We have seen remarkable things today."—Luke 5:26

I'd like to make my case for social media now. I'm a lover of social media, although I know many people are not. It causes us to compare, our phones are rotting our brains, and we're all getting tiny indentions in our pinkies because we're on these contraptions so much. I get it—there are a lot of downsides, and those are just the lighter ones.

But here's what happened last night: I was resting for a moment in bed and decided to look back at a few of my old social media posts and captions, and then at a few of my recent posts and captions. And I smile—it served to remind me of all the ways God has been generous to us in the past.

Then I walked downstairs to where my husband was folding laundry and said, "These are the days. These are some beautiful days." And instead of going to bed discouraged about all we didn't get done, we laughed and felt light in our hearts, grateful for God and His good work.

God is on the move. God is here, God is there—in your ordinary and mundane-looking life. He is working out a million tiny miracles. The Spirit is stirring and shifting the atmosphere. Healing is happening and grace is abounding. Will we capture it? Will we notice it? Will we choose wonder and gratitude and worship, or will we keep our heads down and our backs hunched over, looking at our feet and feeling the discouragement around us?

Wonder isn't dependent on God doing something incredible, because He already is. Wonder is a choice that we make—to take looking at Him and believing in Him too far in all the best ways.

Today, let's choose wonder. Let's choose gratitude. Let's choose worship.

Take Wonder Too Far

Capture one thing you perceive God doing today
and declare with your mouth, your words, maybe
even your social media how good He is and how
grateful you are for the work of His hands.

45 SERVICE

Beloved ones, God has called us to live a life of freedom in the Holy Spirit. But don't view this wonderful freedom as an opportunity to set up a base of operations in the natural realm. Freedom means that we become so completely free of self-indulgence that we become servants of one another, expressing love in all we do.—GALATIANS 5:13 TPT

I never liked sandcastles as a kid. To create one, you have to stay hunched over, and my back is not about that. You get weird tan lines from the way you sit. There is sand *everywhere*—in your hair, in your suit, stuck under your fingernails. Plus, we all know the very worst thing about sandcastles is that they go away. You spend your whole day digging and building and sculpting, and the next morning you have to start again.

Honestly, I know something of sandcastle building in my life because God has shown me I can spend my entire day building my own little kingdom here on earth, or I can use my hands, my hours, my service to build something that will last.

Today, I have the choice: I can spend hours getting dressed and somewhat cute looking, but that goes away when I sleep or work out or basically live too fervently. I can spend my day fluffing pillows and organizing my closet and cleaning my fridge, but that is destroyed the moment other humans enter my domain. (I'm looking at you, Connolly kids.) There are so many things I can do to serve myself, but ultimately they wash away the moment the day gets hectic or when the sun goes down.

But when I spend my hours, my days, my energy serving others? That remains. That love, that affection, that dignity, and that worth that I speak into their lives—all those things impact eternity.

I still do the laundry (and occasionally clean out the fridge), because it keeps us clothed so we can impactfully serve others and not be naked. I still get dressed and take time doing my makeup because a few minutes of maintenance enables me to take it too far when it comes to serving others.

But I know that when the day is done, I don't want to have built a sandcastle of serving myself—I'd rather build something through serving others that will continue to stand, bless, and point to God.

We're free to serve. We get to take it too far. We get to spend our days on something that won't pass away. So why wouldn't we?

Take Service Too Far
Take fifteen minutes and serve someone else today.
Ask God to help you see the fruit of how it impacts
them, glorifies Him, and changes eternity.

46 PURITY

> Who may ascend the mountain of the Lord? Who may stand in his holy place? The one who has clean hands and a pure heart, who does not trust in an idol or swear by a false god.—Psalm 24:3–4

Oh man, when I first came to know God, Psalm 24:3–4 used to do a number on me. Who can ascend the mountain of God? Who can come close to Him? Only the ones with clean hands and pure hearts. What in the world? I'm *out*, bro. I'll never make it! I'm a mess! On my best day I can't come near to God, because even if I can keep my body from massively sinning (I usually can't), my mind and my heart are never fully pure!

I think about reality TV sometimes when I'm praying. I get distracted by online shopping occasionally when I'm reading my Bible. Sometimes at church, out of the corner of my eye I see the girl who hurt me, and then, right there in the throne room of God—look at me: *not pure.*

It took me years to realize that we have to read the Psalms in light of Jesus, in light of the good news that would come hundreds of years after those verses were written. Hebrews 10:19 says that we have confidence to enter the Most Holy Place by the blood of Jesus. His goodness, His righteousness, His purity is our pass to nearness and fellowship with

God. He was the One with the clean hands, the pure heart. He paid the price that we might experience the reward.

Our charge when it comes to purity is not to become pure. Not to muster up what seems unattainable. Not to pretend like we're pure and judge everyone else who has a hard time hiding their impurities. Rather, we've been given the ability to accept the purity that's been written over our lives and into our identities.

We can take purity too far once we realize it's not the secret pass that gets us to God, but it's who we've been made new as—pure sons and daughters, set free to worship and live under the light of His grace. We can take purity too far knowing that grace catches us when impurity slips in and that love compels us to change and grow, never fearing being left out of His kingdom.

Purity isn't our passport to God; it's our purchased identity. Let's take it too far as we align ourselves with who He's made us to be.

Take Purity Too Far

Do something today that agrees with the purity God has
written over your life. Do something that acknowledges
that you don't have to keep yourself pure–you've
already been made pure by the blood of Jesus.

47 JUSTICE

> He has shown you, O mortal, what is good. And what does
> the LORD require of you? To act justly and to love mercy
> and to walk humbly with your God.—MICAH 6:8

Man, there's just no getting around Micah 6:8, is there? What's good?
What should we take too far? God tells us through Micah: Live a just life.
Love mercy—receiving it and giving it to others. Be humble.

Justice is all about rightness and equality. Kingdom-minded justice
is interesting because what we all deserve is death, yet we've received this
ultimate pardon of grace through faith in Jesus Christ, and now we're getting what we don't deserve. You'd think we'd be over the moon to extend
the blessing and generosity we've been handed to others, but instead it's
our sinful nature to sit on them—holding them tightly and pretending
that we've earned them.

We love justice when it's about giving bad guys what they deserve,
but the kingdom has always been about extending undeserved mercy so
we can all experience abundant life, boundless love, and unending grace.

I could write book after book on justice, how I've gotten it wrong
and how we get it confused in this now-and-not-yet kingdom of heavenly
minded people living here on earth. What if, instead, we take it too far

by asking ourselves this one question: *Do I want others to get what they deserve, or do I want them to get what I got—mercy and grace and lavish love?*

If death and condemnation were defeated on the cross of Christ, what does it look like for us to be people of justice? What does it look like for us to take it too far in making our world more equitable—an army of humans receiving grace they can't earn and blessings they don't deserve?

Take Justice Too Far

Ask God to give you new ideas to see justice today. Instead of trying to be the judge, ask Him if there is a way you can help someone else experience a more equitable life here on earth.

48 HUMILITY

"If my people, who are called by my name, will humble themselves and pray and seek my face and turn from their wicked ways, then I will hear from heaven, and I will forgive their sin and will heal their land."—2 Chronicles 7:14

It was my freshman year in college and my first few months on staff at a local church. We'd had some kind of gathering that night, and I had come home and gotten ready for bed. My makeup was off and I was settling in when my cell phone rang. It was my brother-in-law, who worked with me at the church, and he wanted to talk. He was downstairs at my dorm. Why was my brother-in-law coming to see me at 11 p.m. unless he had bad news?

He sat me down to tell me how broken and discouraged he was over my pride lately. Maybe it was the staff job at church, maybe it was leadership, but I was exhibiting no signs of humility—and he knew that wasn't who God made me to be. I wasn't mad or all that combative—I knew he was right. I'd been a mess lately.

Since then, no one has sat me down to tell me how prideful I am. It's not because I'm particularly humble but because I feel like maybe I've learned to spot the look on someone's face when I've stepped over the line, and I can move back or apologize for my lack of humility. Because it still happens, and I still find myself tripping over my own ego.

This verse about humility and God's subsequent healing has also played in my mind for years when I've felt pride puffing me up and pulling things apart. And I have an idea: in 2 Chronicles 7:14 God says that if His people will humble themselves, He'll heal their land. The Holy Spirit always reminds me of this: What if humbling yourself is accepting healing? What if the biggest blessing of all for walking in humility is just experiencing the fruit of having a right understanding of ourselves, our King, and the other humans He also loves?

What if there is an automatic healing in our lives that takes place when we allow ourselves to be humbled—just because we're not prideful and prickly and painful to be around any longer? And if so, wouldn't we take humility too far—to experience the most of Him that we can and allow others to do the same? We could see humility as a gift we get to access rather than a punishment we must endure.

Take Humility Too Far

Take a moment to agree with who God has made you to
be–humbled and ready to let Him get all the glory.

49 ABIDE

"You are already clean because of the word which I have spoken to you. Abide in Me, and I in you."—John 15:3–4 NKJV

In a chapter of the Bible on abiding, in a section of Scripture that is all about planting and vines and garden imagery, I've always found it so interesting that Jesus says, "You are already clean."

Also, it's interesting that He says you're already clean "because of the *word which I have spoken*." Man, I wish it worked like that for my kids. What if when they were filthy, I could just look at them and say, "*Clean!*"? I'd forgo the entire bath/shower debate, I wouldn't have to wash eighteen towels because they refuse to use just one, and I wouldn't have to spend thirty dollars a month on body wash because my youngest insists on using half a bottle when I'm not looking.

What would you do or not do if you could get clean with just a word? How would your life change if you could have everything be perfectly tidy and acceptable just by speaking it into being and not lifting a finger? How much more rest and relaxation would be in your days?

Spiritually, what if you were sanctified, justified, given grace, given gifts, made whole, made new, rescued, redeemed, and set on firm standing with God just by Him saying so?

Well . . . all of God's Word speaks to the truth that that's how it is for you. You're who you are in Christ, you've been given this amazing freedom and holy identity, and you're a recipient of His mercy and grace—just because on the cross Christ said, "It is finished" (John 19:30).

So now we have a picture of why these verses go together. If physically we didn't have to clean our houses, our bodies, our cars, or our children, we know we'd have more physical rest. If spiritually we are not responsible for the saving and sanctifying but rather Jesus is doing the heavy lifting, *true abiding* is ours for the taking.

We can take a deep breath. We can relax. We can rest. We can abide. And we can take it too far because He's not only made it possible but reminded us throughout His Word that what He wants most is for us to draw near and to be with Him rather than toil and try to earn our way to Him. We can remain in His presence without earning our keep.

Take Abiding Too Far

Today in your time with God, just sit with Him.
Just remain—in silence, in quiet, without trying
to get better or earn your place there.

50 HONOR

"Whoever serves me must follow me; and where I am, my servant also will be. My Father will honor the one who serves me."—John 12:26

When I think about honor, I think about standing up when someone enters the room. I feel like this cultural practice has slowed way down in the past few decades, and I'm not sure whether that's a good or a bad thing. But now it's so infrequent that when it does happen, we really take notice: this is someone who deserves honor.

A dignitary, an elder we respect, our boss—these are people who might bring us to our feet when they enter our presence. The gesture is transactional; it's based on something they bring to the table—even if they haven't earned the honor. We give them worldly honor because on earth they have been ascribed more value or glory for some particular reason.

What's interesting about worldly honor is that it always keeps us from relational intimacy. You don't cuddle up next to the person you respect the most or pour out your heart to the politician who just entered the room. The more we honor and revere someone on earth, the more likely it is that we'll be kept from close contact with that person. And this is where kingdom honor takes a massive turn away from the ways of this world.

First, God gives out honor through Jesus—not transactionally but rather by transposing His affections for His Son onto us, covering us with His shed blood, and showering His love, grace, and mercy on us. We follow Jesus, and we're in—no matter our future transgressions or our past mistakes. We are bestowed honor we don't deserve from a God who gives it freely.

And the honor that we give Him back is nothing like the world in that the more praise and respect and reverence we pour His way, the nearer we are to Him. Once we honor Him as Lord and treat Him that way, we're not kept far off but brought near, our intimacy with Him purchased and procured, once again, by Jesus.

May we take honor too far, the way God does—respecting and revering the children He loves but also acknowledging that no one is too messy to be kept from Him. May we draw close to others as we encourage them to perceive just how close He has come for all of us.

Take Honor Too Far
Honor God today by honoring another
human the way He would. Take it too far by
respecting that person *and* drawing near.

51 FRIENDSHIP

"I no longer call you servants, because a servant does not know his master's business. Instead, I have called you friends, for everything that I learned from my Father I have made known to you."—John 15:15

I had to go to a wedding a few months ago, and I was feeling a little insecure. I didn't like what I had to wear, didn't love how I looked, and I wasn't particularly good friends with a lot of the women there. Well, to speak plainly, I felt rejected and left out by a handful of the women who would be attending. I wanted to celebrate my friend getting married, and I wanted to believe that abundance was for me, but I just felt kind of lackluster. I tried to give the "This isn't about you, so forget your yucky feelings" talk to myself, but it didn't really help.

I was speaking with another friend who said, "Instead of telling yourself that all those insecure feelings don't matter, why don't you focus on what you bring to the table. Ask God to help you be aware of what you do have every time you enter a room or begin a conversation."

I loved that idea because it's so positive and because it sent me to the throne room of my Father for clarity and wisdom, and here's what I came back with: What I bring to the table is not how I look; it's not who loves me; it's not my gifts or my accolades or the amount that I can get done in a day. What I bring to every room, every relationship, and every interaction I have with other humans is the fact that I am a friend of God. And because I am a friend of God, I have access to hope, security, compassion, empathy, freedom, trust, grace, and love. He gives generously to me what I don't deserve, and I am able to share that with others.

When we struggle with friendship, I find so often we're asking the question, What do I even bring to the table? And man, we'll do so much better if we don't try to fake our way into that answer or try to seem like we're someone we're not. We'll do much better in life and in love if we take our friendship with God too far, take it for every ounce of abundance that it's worth, and then exuberantly give that same friendship to those He's placed in our lives.

We take friendship too far by taking our friendship with God seriously and by believing what He's said to us and about us.

Take Friendship Too Far

Take a moment to treat God like your friend since He's called Himself just that (John 15:14). Then plan one interaction today with a human friend where you can give generously from what He's extended to you.

52 ENDURANCE

May the God who gives endurance and encouragement give you
the same attitude of mind toward each other that Christ Jesus
had, so that with one mind and one voice you may glorify the
God and Father of our Lord Jesus Christ.—Romans 15:5–6

When I was growing up, my stepdad had a funny saying that was super
obnoxious to me as a kid yet probably helpful in actually becoming an
adult. Isn't it interesting that sometimes it's the obnoxious pieces of wisdom that are the most beneficial?

He used to ask, "Is it pain or irritation?"

If I stubbed my toe and was screaming my head off, he'd gently ask,
"Pain or irritation?" Earache: "Pain or irritation?" Most of the time I'd
grumble back, "Irrrrrritatttttion." But on the rare occasions I was really
injured, I'd be able to tell him, "Pain." And he'd know I was serious. The
qualifying process helped me evaluate what was happening and respond
accordingly, something my stepdad, the son of a doctor, knew well. Slowing
down to evaluate what we're experiencing helps us get our bearings and
gives us vision for what we need to do to alleviate any pressure or pain.

I've started to play a similar game with physiological pain, irritation, or pressure. The game I now play in my head is "Inconvenience or

endurance?" Is this problem that I'm currently encountering going to be only an inconvenience in my life, *or* am I going to allow God to work in and through me to make it an event that increases my endurance for the long haul? Essentially, I'm asking, "Is this going to be temporary pain, or is it going to be used for permanent growth?"

The Word of God literally never promises an easy life. In fact, it promises the opposite: in this world you will have *trouble* (John 16:33). Heartache, pain, discomfort, loss, death, and general irritation abound on earth. But God makes a way for us to be united with Christ and to grow in the attitudes and expressions that He offers. We can become more patient, more compassionate, more loving, more generous—all while we're hurting. Our inconveniences can instead become what aid in our endurance. And that is some serious revitalization that we couldn't do on our own.

Take Endurance Too Far

Today, pick one inconvenience and ask God how He is increasing your capacity to endure it. Take it too far and worship Him in the midst of the trial–no matter how big or small–and see your perspective shift.

53 REVERENCE

Then He said, "Do not come near here; remove your sandals from your feet, for the place on which you are standing is holy ground."—Exodus 3:5 NASB

Of all the scenes I'd like to see replayed in heaven, this is one for sure: "God, can I see the replay of the parting of the Red Sea? Also, creation—maybe in hyperspeed? I'd love to see when resurrected Jesus made the disciples breakfast, and—*oh yeah*—is there any way to get a replay of Moses seeing the burning bush?"

Exodus 3:5 is surely one of our favorite references to reverence in the Bible. The booming voice of the Father interjects in the middle of the mundane, and God declares the place Moses stands is holy. I've done a lot of research about the *why* behind Him telling Moses to take off his shoes because that line in particular is just a little interesting. We'll know more when we're with God in heaven, I'm assured, but theologians conjecture that the shoe removal has to do with reverence and humility. I'm just so grateful that when we show reverence to God, we don't have to place more barriers between Him and us.

I'm so grateful that reverence doesn't have anything to do with adding layers or hiding, but has everything to do with stripping down to show what we're really working with. I'm so thankful that as we see God even more clearly in His perfect power, as we grow in reverence of who He really is and what He can do, His instructions are not for us to dress ourselves up or put on costumes.

Reverence is not disengaging because we assume God doesn't think we're worthy. It isn't pretending to be someone we're not. Reverence isn't making ourselves look tidier, and it isn't puffing ourselves up to seem better than we are.

Reverence, coupled with humility, acknowledges that God is all-powerful and all-loving. Reverence acknowledges that He's otherworldly and all-encompassing, but He still wants to commune and communicate with us. May we take reverence too far, stripping off pretense and taking off our shoes in His presence. May we come boldly and humbly to the throne room of grace, just as we are, expecting Him to be who only He can be.

Take Reverence Too Far

What would it look like to take off your shoes today? To acknowledge God's holiness and, in response, reverently and humbly be a little more honest in His presence about who you are?

54 AVAILABLE

"Am I not a God near at hand"—God's Decree—"and not a God far off? Can anyone hide out in a corner where I can't see him?" God's Decree. "Am I not present everywhere, whether seen or unseen?" God's Decree.—JEREMIAH 23:23–24 MSG

I see a professional Christian counselor a couple of times a month, and there is no shame in my game. God has used counseling mightily in my life to keep me healthy and keep me using all I've got to serve and love my people well.

However, something that was a little hard to get used to about counseling was this: my counselor and I don't have an equitable relationship in regard to how we listen to and serve one another. Meaning, I don't have to ask her how she's doing or how she's feeling; in fact, even if I do, it's not appropriate for her to take our time to tell me. Our relationship has individual roles, and while we're equally valuable, she's the one leading this shebang. I just show up and follow her lead to a healthier me.

My counselor is available to me in ways that I cannot reciprocate, because she does not need me to be available to her. God is like that too. Sometimes we get tripped up by His continual and eternal openness to us. We forget that He isn't bound by our limitations or His expectations of us.

He lives outside the limits of human time and space because He created both. When He gives us attention, it isn't taking His energy from another person or project—because His attention, availability, and capacity are literally limitless.

As we assess our own availability, we have to acknowledge that we're under human constraints. We can't be in two places at once, much less everywhere at once. We do have a finite level of energy and a limited capacity of how much we can do, *but* . . . we're also made in God's image and given His power to love and serve others, and it can be incredibly helpful for us to ask Him to increase our capacity to be available. He'll help us be more available for those we're meant to serve, and He'll also help us stop limiting how much we think we can give when it comes to the good of others and the glory of God.

Take Availability Too Far

Prayerfully create a short list of people you know
God has called you to be available for. Ask Him
to give you the capacity and energy to serve them
and to be a reflection of His love for them.

55 DISCERNMENT

Your commandment makes me wiser than my enemies, for it is ever with me. I have more understanding than all my teachers, for your testimonies are my meditation. I understand more than the aged, for I keep your precepts. I hold back my feet from every evil way, in order to keep your word. I do not turn aside from your rules, for you have taught me. How sweet are your words to my taste, sweeter than honey to my mouth!—Psalm 119:98–103 ESV

I was reading Psalm 119 the other day and just had to giggle. Can you imagine one of us saying this today? Picture me meeting up with a friend after Bible study, sipping my coffee, and saying something like, "I am genuinely so much smarter than all the people who hate me, because of the Bible. Even my leaders at Bible study—I understand more than they do! I just think all day about how God has shown up and let that simmer in my heart till I'm super faith-filled. Even older women, I'm smarter than them—mostly just because I obey Scripture! I'm not tempted to sin; God's Word is too good." Can you even imagine?

But the thing is—I don't think the psalmist is way out of line with these words. I don't think he's boasting in his power but in the discernment and insight that come from studying God's Word. I think he's letting us know that when we read the Word and truly let it simmer in our hearts, it changes us. It gives us direction. It gives us insight.

I don't think we'd be loving each other well if we said, "Want discernment? Here's a five-step plan!" Rather, I think the wisest thing we can encourage one another with is this: if we want to take discernment too far, if we want to take God for all that He's worth, we'll simply agree that He *already* has provided insight in His Word and expect, in faith, that He is going to continue to give it.

Sometimes I'll just write down a list of questions or decisions I need to make and keep it tucked in my Bible. And the best thing I can do to gain discernment is to (a) keep reading His Word and (b) keep expecting that He's going to give me the wisdom to make a decision and the grace to move forward even if I make the wrong one.

Take discernment too far today by understanding that God has already given it. Run to the Word of God and run into His presence, believing He'll answer your every question.

Take Discernment Too Far

Make a short list of decisions you need to make or questions
you've got for God. Read His Word. Ask Him to help,
and ask Him for the faith to trust that He will.

56 DEPTH

> He reveals deep and hidden things; he knows what lies in
> darkness, and light dwells with him.—Daniel 2:22

Oh, how I can take depth too far. I woke up like this. I was born like this. I can't even slightly help it.

True story: when I was a kid, I used to get stuck in front of the mirror for hours—not primping and perfecting my hair, but staring at the indentation over my lips and below my nose and wondering what its function was.

In case you're curious, it's called a philtrum, and it's believed to have developed to help with our sense of smell, but it has no function in modern-day life. Jewish mystics believe it's where the angels touch babies just before they're born to clear them of all memory of the miraculous and divine things they've been shown in utero. Deep, huh? I bet you'll never look at that little indentation above your lip the same again, right?

Here's the thing about going deep. Whether we're asking universally puzzling questions or bringing the darkest parts of our lives to the table to ask for help, I think it's helpful to know that even when other humans can't or won't keep up, God is ready to go deep.

In fact, He's already there. He created the deep. He formed it. The mysterious is His craftsmanship; the hard problems that seem unsolvable have already been worked out in His economy of time. The darkest pits of sin and pain are not hidden from Him, and He's carefully created a rescue plan to pull those whom He loves out of them. He's not scared of the dark; He's not scared of the deep.

So take it too far, your dive into things of depth. Ask big questions, acknowledge large problems, and poke around in the dark. But know, without a shadow of a doubt, that the Spirit of God is with you and bringing the light. Don't go alone; ask Him to guide you. He knows the way.

Take Depth Too Far

Is there an area of depth you've been avoiding?
Ask God to go with you and light up your steps
as you move toward it. Have you been feeling like
you have to explore the caves of pain and darkness
alone? Remember that He's by your side.

57 HOLINESS

> But you are a chosen people, a royal priesthood, a holy nation, God's special possession, that you may declare the praises of him who called you out of darkness into his wonderful light.—1 Peter 2:9

I was at a leadership conference in college when I first heard a Bible teacher say, "You're as holy right now as you'll ever be." I watched a ripple of confusion and flustering spread through the room as the words hit. *Is that theologically correct? Hmm . . .*

Later I followed up with a pastor I respected, and he confirmed: it didn't *sound* right to our human ears, but scripturally, if we believe Jesus paid the price for our sin, and by grace, through faith, we put our trust in Him—yeah, He's made us new. He's made us *holy*.

I wrote an entire book (*Dance Stand Run*) around this one idea: by grace through faith, God has made me holy, and I just get to agree with that. I don't have to earn it or work my way toward it. And that kind of grace should cause me to dance in celebration, stand my holy ground, and run on mission.

I think there are two guidelines that will help us if we're going to approach this God-given characteristic with gusto:

1. We should talk about our holiness and no one else's. When we start talking about other people's holiness and whether or not they're living as the people God has made them to be, we put ourselves in God's spot, and that's not a good look.

2. We should always remember that holiness is not about becoming someone else but agreeing with who God has already made us to be. And when we take it too far, we're not earning our place in His family but taking our place in the kingdom that Jesus died to have us in.

You're holy if you're a part of the family of God; there's no getting around it. And that means you have proximity to God, the privileges of His kingdom, and the power of the Holy Spirit at your disposal. Of all the things we've been handed, man, is this ever a beautiful and gracious one.

Take Holiness Too Far
Answer this one question: How would my day change
if I agreed that I've been made holy by God?

58 HEALING

Is anyone among you sick? Let them call the elders of the church to pray over them and anoint them with oil in the name of the Lord. And the prayer offered in faith will make the sick person well; the Lord will raise them up. If they have sinned, they will be forgiven.—JAMES 5:14–15

What do you want God to say to you when you get to heaven? I mean, what do you *even think* that will be like? I confess I used to read the Left Behind books over and over and over again—because I just love picturing what interacting with Jesus will be like for all eternity.

I know we're all hoping for the "Well done, good and faithful servant!" (See Matthew 25:14–30.) I'm there too. And I know I'm going to be overcome with Jesus' glory in a way that I can't even imagine right now. Scripture informs me that when I really see Him, when I really understand, I'm going to want to worship Him for eternity (read Revelation 5:11–14), and that sounds amazing. Unimaginable, but amazing.

But for the last few years I've had this nagging feeling, and I can kind of picture Him with a gentle smile on His face, saying, "I wish you'd taken My Word, friend. I wish you'd believed all that I said!"

One subject that really makes me feel that way is healing. So much of Scripture points to the fact that Jesus physically heals, and so little of my life leans on that truth.

A few years ago, I was diagnosed with an autoimmune disease, and I can promise you I've spent many, many more hours at the doctor than I have on my knees, begging for healing. I don't feel shame about that, but I do wonder if I'm missing out on all that Jesus has to offer. I don't want to reach eternity to have Him say, "Sister! I had so much more for you on earth!"

We all know that in heaven there will be no pain (hallelujah!), but that means that in heaven, there won't be continued opportunities to experience Jesus' physical healing. Which means . . . now is our chance to take Him at His Word.

Let's take it too far—with our hopes in Him and not in the healing.

Take Healing Too Far

A headache, cancer, a private concern–whatever needs
healing in your life, just ask Him today. Take it too far
and remind Him that He has given you permission.

59 LIGHT

For you were once darkness, but now you are light in the Lord. Live
as children of light (for the fruit of the light consists in all goodness,
righteousness and truth) and find out what pleases the Lord. Have
nothing to do with the fruitless deeds of darkness, but rather expose
them. It is shameful even to mention what the disobedient do in
secret. But everything exposed by the light becomes visible—and
everything that is illuminated becomes a light.—Ephesians 5:8–13

My husband and I went to the beach in the dark last night and just . . .
looked. The sight of the black sky and the bright stars was jarring. Scary,
almost. Because God is big and mysterious and risky, and He made *all*
this. He holds *all* of this up. I can't even fathom His size, His power, and
the darkness that's out there. But I looked.

Today, as I walked outside, I thought, *Honestly, the light is as jarring
as the dark.* It's exposing. It's obnoxiously honest. The light calls me to
stand, to run, to *wake up*! It reminds me of who I am in the wake of God's
shining.

We don't have to be scared. We can dance in the light knowing
God's grace is on us. We can run into the night, powered by His grace,
and can grab others and show them who He is and how much He loves

us. We don't have to be scared of either the light or the dark. We don't have to hide.

What are you keeping hidden from God or humans? What are you covering up and hoping they won't see? What would happen if the light of God got ahold of your darkness? Increased exposure to the dark will not make us braver, but it will make us bitter. And hiding from the light won't keep us safe; instead, it will keep us scared. The light is where we were made to run; it's who we are; it's what we were purchased for.

Take Living in the Light Too Far
Take some time with God today and bring one
thing into the light. One confession, one sin,
one dream or desire you may be hiding.

60 BEAUTY

He has made everything beautiful in its time.—Ecclesiastes 3:11

When I studied history in school and got to the Age of Enlightenment and even the Renaissance, what always struck me is this strange belief that God and art, God and growth, even God and beauty are at war. It's surely a lie implanted by the enemy, and I'm sure those both inside and outside the church have helped to make it seem like a fact, but goodness gracious, is it damaging! Our view of God is skewed when we think of Him as not being concerned with beauty or not being the supplier of it, and our experience is limited when we separate the Creator from His very good creation.

When I see some of the works of art that came out of that time—statues, murals, paintings—I can't help but think how enjoyable it must have been for the Spirit of God to work in and through the hands of those artisans. I know that humans don't come by those gifts on their own. When I see the Grand Canyon or Yosemite or the ocean or a sunset or a really interesting flower, I know that God loves and creates and uses beauty to bring Himself glory *and* to make our lives more joy-filled.

Perhaps the most important way we can take beauty too far is by remembering that God is the Author of beauty; He loves it enough to give it away, and we give Him credit when we partake of it or partner with Him to create it.

Beauty is God's good idea. Let's enjoy it. Let's seek to establish it in our spaces. Let's remember that it was His idea, and it is His power that works all the good and worthy things that fill our lives.

Take Beauty Too Far
Take it too far today by slowing down, enjoying something beautiful, and thanking God for making it. Ask Him how you can use what you've got to bring a little beauty to your world today.

61 CURIOSITY

I meditate on all your works and consider what
your hands have done.—PSALM 143:5

Let's get it straight from the get-go: God is not curious. Curiosity comes from a lack of knowledge and an openness, a longing for more, and thank goodness God knows everything. He doesn't have a lack of knowledge, which is great news for us. Nothing is a surprise to Him; nothing is a mystery He can't quite put His finger on or a problem He can't solve. He isn't curious, because He's holy and all-knowing.

Yet, in His good and perfect will, He did *not* make us all-knowing. First Corinthians 13:12 says that we know in part, but one day we'll know in full. God gives us His Word, His Spirit. He gives us prophecy and words of encouragement from one another. He's giving us little snippets and vision of what He's up to—but we don't see the whole picture.

Is acting on our curiosity a worthy endeavor? Or is it better that we just keep to what we know and see right now? Should we simply be grateful for the knowledge that we currently possess and keep our heads down until we die or Jesus comes back?

I vote no. And I perceive that most of Scripture points to no; we shouldn't just take the limited knowledge we're working with right now and settle in. Instead, we get to consider God's works and meditate on His Word. We get to grow, to learn, to repent, to be shifted. We get to go and see and learn and mess up and try again. We get to dive into literal caves to see what God created and explore the figurative caverns of life, looking for Him in every little nook and cranny.

We get to be curious because curiosity says there is more knowledge out there for us, and that is ultimately a humble and open state to live in. We get to be curious because that makes us unblocked vessels—recipients ready to experience more of God's beauty, grace, wisdom, power, and presence.

Let's take it too far. Let's see what else is out there. Let's remember that God will guide us and grace us with His wisdom when we ask for it. Let's be curious! Curiosity may have killed the cat, but it humbles the human, and that sounds amazing.

Take Curiosity Too Far

Make a quick list of two or three things you're curious about and submit them to the Lord. Check back on the list in a few weeks and see if He has surprised you or revealed Himself to you in some new ways.

62 GIVING

In everything I did, I showed you that by this kind of hard work we must help the weak, remembering the words the Lord Jesus himself said: "It is more blessed to give than to receive."—Acts 20:35

Here's what I love about God: He doesn't just want us to *be* good; He wants us to *have* good. He doesn't just want good *from* us; He wants it *for* us. And so He gives us this knowledge that sets us up for a life of abundance and joy and freedom for us to give it all away.

You might be saying, "Hold on one second, Jess Connolly. God doesn't say give it *all* away." And to that, I would remind you that this book isn't called *Mediocrity: Do Just Enough to Get By*. It's not called *The Middle Road: Keep It Average to Experience the Same Thing Everyone Else Does*. It's called *Take It Too Far: Abundant Life, Boundless Love, Unending Grace*. We're here for the extra mile. We're here for the second helping. We're here to take God's Word so seriously that people accuse us of being over-the-top.

Maybe you can't give it all away, but could you try? Maybe you're scared to give it all away, but could you test and see how God might show up? And what is it that we're giving away? Maybe we should ask what it is that God has encouraged us to hold on to. What has He commanded us to keep for ourselves, to bury and not to share? What has He told us to hoard and be selfish with?

Oh. Nothing. He's been generous with us, giving us *everything*. Money, provision, love, wisdom, His presence, purpose, healing, power, blessings, health, worth, family, community, coffee, hope, freedom, coffee (that's right; it's in there twice), and *so many other things*. And He's generous and giving because it brings Him glory and because it blesses Him to do so.

We can sit on our hands and our gifts and make excuses for what we can't give away, or we can take it too far—for His glory, for the good of others, and for the blessing of our own selves. I don't know about you, but I'm trying to get blessed today. I'm trying to take it too far.

Take Giving Too Far
Ask God for wisdom about one physical thing
you can give away today, one emotional thing
you can give away today, and one spiritual
thing you can give away today. Then do it!

63 HOSPITALITY

Do not forget to show hospitality to strangers, for by so doing some people
have shown hospitality to angels without knowing it.—Hebrews 13:2

I believe there are three distinct words and ideas that we often get mixed
up: hosting, entertaining, and hospitality. Let's look at the difference.

Hosting is having something or someone at your home or residence.
We're having community group? I'll host! I'll make sure my floors are
swept and maybe have a few extra soda waters on hand. I can make coffee too. People walk away from their host grateful that there was space
for them.

Entertaining is putting on a show. Now, I don't mean that you're
sitting everyone down and doing some Mariah Carey karaoke, but it does
mean there is some delight and entertainment involved. You're putting
care into the little details that show you've got a beautiful space. The
votives match the napkins, or the coffee bar is just 110 percent cute.
People walk away from being entertained aware of just how awesome you
are. Their attention is on you and your greatness.

Hospitality is a mixture of hosting and entertaining, where the focus
is on the good of those you're letting in your home. If entertaining is
saying, "Here I am!" then hospitality is saying, "There you are!" Maybe

the details are thought out, but not for the glory of the one hosting, but rather, for the intentionality of the occasion and the blessing of the attendee. People walk away from true Christ-centered hospitality feeling loved and seen, which mirrors God's affection and attention toward them.

You don't have to be great at decorating to be hospitable, and you absolutely don't have to have the most beautiful home. You don't need to be a gourmet chef or have the cutest utensils. To be hospitable we just need the availability that hosts have, and we can throw in some of the spice and intentionality of entertaining with God's glory and the good of others at the forefront of our minds to really take it too far. We get to pause and ask God, "How can I mirror Your grace, goodness, love, and mercy to the people who are entering my home, my space, my presence today? How can I be hospitable and thus be like You to those who need it most?"

Take Hospitality Too Far

Plan an event! It doesn't have to be elaborate. It doesn't have to involve a lot of people. Just invite over a handful of folks and love them like Jesus would for a morning or an afternoon. Serve them coffee–or a three-course meal.

64 HUMOR

To everything there is a season, a time for every purpose under heaven. . . . a time to weep, and a time to laugh. —Ecclesiastes 3:1, 4 NKJV

I once heard a teaching on God being funny. The Bible teacher said that in Genesis, after Adam and Eve sinned and hid from God, we saw clear proof of God's humor when He asked them where they were. Picture Him, like a mom who can clearly see her kids hiding behind the curtain, saying their names in a silly and slightly taunting voice.

I really doubt that God was being silly and humorous then, but I am fairly certain God is funny. To be honest, here's how I know: I'm made in His image, and all of my best parts and good gifts are from Him. And I think I'm pretty stinking funny. It doesn't matter if other people do, right? I know that I absolutely love to laugh, and I've experienced what can only be God's joy and comfort in the midst of laughter. Plus, there are tons of biblical references to laughter, joy, and lighthearted celebration. So how in the world do we take humor too far? Here are a few ideas:

- *We keep our humor from being hurtful to others.* There's so much to laugh at without laughing at others' expense. If we want to experience true lightness, we won't pull others into a dark space with our humor.

- *We keep our humor in the light.* If we don't joke about stuff we'd be embarrassed to say to our pastor or our parents, we're usually in a good spot. (FYI, my husband is my pastor, and no one makes me laugh more than he does.)
- *We invite God into our times of laughter.* Often, if we're at dinner with friends, before the meal I'll pray for God to help us enjoy it, and I'll also tell Him that I want Him to enjoy it too! It helps me remember that He goes with me and I want to go with Him.

Let's take it too far and fight back the lie that says believers' lives have to be all about books written decades ago and serious talk. We serve the God who created laughter.

Take Humor Too Far

I dare you to play a board game or a card game with a few
kids. Playing games with kids reminds me that good,
clean fun is a great idea, and humor is all around.

65 FAVOR

The LORD will guide you always; he will satisfy your needs in a sun-scorched land and will strengthen your frame. You will be like a well-watered garden, like a spring whose waters never fail.—ISAIAH 58:11

Did you know that writing books isn't just about writing books? It's often about telling people that you write books, so they know that you write books and buy said books, so you keep your job. And sometimes it's about asking other people to tell people that you wrote the book so their people know, so they buy the books, so you keep your job.

You get this, I'm sure, in your line of work. If you're a nanny, you need references. If you're a chef or a professional organizer or a barista or an administrative assistant, it helps when other people vouch for you that you're good at your job. And in seasons when you really need people to do that, it can feel a little hectic, and maybe even like you're trying to perform for favor. I wonder if in your job or in your life, you've had that one person in mind who could vouch for you . . . the one person who would change everything. If that person showed your work just a little affection and attention, it would blow up. Or so it seems, right?

A few years ago, in one of those seasons when I needed people to tell other people about my book, and particularly when I was feeling a little desperate about it, God put something in my spirit so incredibly clear it almost felt audible. He said, "No one's approval or lack thereof can speed up or thwart My plan for your life."

There is no human who could ever possibly bring favor like God. We think certain people could change everything for the better or break it all down with their disapproval of us, but God is so much bigger than that. He's so much better than that. And His favor is always coming toward you, working out His best for you.

Thank God for the earthly favor He may give you, but take the eternal and spiritual favor you've been given too far. Because when we stop seeing people as tools and stepping-stones and signs that we're okay, we're freed up to pay favor forward, lavishly loving others—no matter what comes our way.

Take Favor Too Far

List three ways God has met your needs in
the last week. Then list three ways that you're
asking Him to help in the week to come.

66 GRACE

But he said to me, "My grace is sufficient for you, for my power is made perfect in weakness." Therefore I will boast all the more gladly about my weaknesses, so that Christ's power may rest on me.—2 Corinthians 12:9

Want to change the world? Keep reading.

The world tells us that our weaknesses are for hiding, stuffing, fixing, and pretending as if they don't exist. But . . . the kingdom. But . . . grace. But . . . Jesus. He always has a better plan. So in this beautiful, upside-down, grace-filled, and abundant relationship we have with Him, instead of asking us to hide, He invites us to let our weaknesses hit the air so they can be shifted and changed and instead become points of entry for the power of God to change the world.

Your weaknesses are not a liability to the kingdom of God, and there is no skeleton in the closet or hidden trait in your being that would shock Him or cause Him to stop coming toward you in grace. All of you is loved, all of you is held, everything is redeemable, and the rest of your life is dependent on *His* capacity, not on your ability to cover up who you are or how you've been made.

Do you want a power-filled life? Do you want a life where the power of God gets stuff done and changes the world? Then start allowing those weaknesses to shine so grace can do its good work in you and through you.

Take it too far and let God extend His grace to you. Stop trying to hide, and stop trying to blame, and stop trying to pretend you don't need it. And while you're at it, hand some to your friend. She's struggling and needs the grace too.

Take Grace Too Far

What can you allow God to forgive you for today?
What have you been hiding from Him? How can
you extend grace to just one other person?

67 NURTURING

Because of the Lord's great love we are not consumed, for
his compassions never fail. They are new every morning;
great is your faithfulness.—Lamentations 3:22–23

My friend Cheryl is an incredible pastor and an amazing mother. She
doesn't actually have any biological children, but she has spiritually moth-
ered countless men and women in her decades of ministry. The other day
I asked her to trace the similarities between mothering and pastoring, and
she pointed toward a nurturing spirit, which I totally agree with. Both
pastoring and mothering take nurturing, for sure.

She asked me if I saw those two things connecting in myself, regarding my call to both pastoring and mothering, and I had to admit to her
that it's my lack of natural ability to nurture that has always made me feel
insecure as a mother and also as a minister of the gospel.

Cheryl was quick to point out that my "lack of a natural ability to
nurture" must be a lie since I'm made in the image of God and since
He's clearly called me to both motherhood and ministry. Isn't that like
the enemy, that stupid old liar, to convince us we can't do the very thing
we're already doing? To convince us we're not like God even though He's
placed His compassion and sense of nurturing in us?

Here's what I know: believing that God has given us the capacity for something often makes it much more enjoyable. Lately I've seen my love for motherhood growing, and it's not because I'm doing it perfectly or better or different. I love being a mom because it's one more area where I experience God's power being made perfect in my weakness when I *just show up* and believe He's placed me there on purpose. And I enjoy it more because I believe that He'll equip me to fulfill the roles where He's already placed me.

Take Nurturing Too Far

Whether you're a mother or a pastor or neither, how can you agree today that God has made you nurturing? Do you need to take it too far and believe that you can mother even if you've never had biological children? That you can shepherd people even if you haven't been ordained?

68 WORK

"But seek first his kingdom and his righteousness, and all these things will be given to you as well."—Matthew 6:33

A few years ago, a friend and I were dreaming about our schedules and how to structure our weeks for the most abundant living, and we decided to make an outline of what our ideal day looked like. We both became quiet and got to dreaming and then showed each other, in detail, what an ideal day in our life would look like. Hers sounded awesome (a day at the beach with a good book!), but it was different from mine in this one way: I would definitely work on my best dream day. Maybe not nine hours and maybe not on humdrum emails, but you better believe I'd love to write, lead, and maybe even study for teaching on my ideal day. I adore my job, the strategizing and working on my calendar to make the most of my time. I enjoy the feeling that pulses through my fingertips when I set them on the keys on my laptop for the first time in the morning. You may have just visibly smiled when you read that because it resonates with you, or maybe you laughed—or grimaced. I am astounded and grateful that God's made us all so different.

I love to work. So how do I know when I'm taking work too far for the glory of God rather than because I want to get ahead? Matthew 6:33. Am I building God's kingdom or mine?

If I'm building my kingdom, I get famous; I get wealthy; I get ahead; I get the glory. If I'm building my kingdom, I'm scared to rest; I spin and strive. But if I'm building His kingdom, He gets more famous, other people get served, and the resources I earn are used to help serve others. If I'm building His kingdom, I know I have to do it His way, going slowly, taking breaks, experiencing Him, and worshiping and resting as I go.

As with every single topic we've covered in this book, we can take it too far in a damaging way if it's not God's glory and kingdom that we're aimed at. But oh, man, when we're pointed at Him and asking Him what He wants, we are safe and encouraged to work unto the Lord. To work hard, to work with purpose, to work on our best days because we just can't wait to, because it's all for His fame and the good of others. And that is a beautiful thing.

Take Work Too Far

Work hard today! Not because you have to but because you get to! Wash the dishes with gusto; send the email with energy; do the laundry with joy. Work unto the Lord, and take it too far. This is kingdom work you're doing!

69 SINCERITY

In Christ we speak before God with sincerity, as
those sent from God.—2 CORINTHIANS 2:17

Does God ever ask you hard questions? I find that every so often, He plants one in my heart that really makes me pause and listen, reflect, and often repent. Recently He asked me, "Do you want to love people, or do you want to *seem* like you love people?"

Well, okay, Father. Way to cut to the quick.

The truth is that sincerely wanting good for others, sincerely loving others, sincerely speaking life and truth to others is one direction. You can point in that direction, fall off the path, get off track, hop back on the path, and still end up in a really good spot.

But if your aim is to appear as though you love other people, that's an entirely different direction on the map, and if you point that way initially, you'll end up somewhere that has nothing to do with loving people. I say this with all the transparency and vulnerability of someone who made the mistake of trying to seem like I loved people for a few years and ended up somewhere I never meant to be.

The main difference is where we aim, who we're trying to please, and whether we're comfortable being insincere. The way to the place I want to go looks a lot like this simple prayer: *God, help me want to love others. Help me want to please You. Make me uncomfortable and convicted when I'm being insincere.*

I've found that not only is God faithful to ask really hard questions; He's also faithful to come through when I ask Him to make me uncomfortable or convicted. He loves a heart willing to be corrected, and He shows up every time.

We can take it too far with our sincerity, which starts inwardly, quietly, and honestly in our hearts. God will give us the direction to go and make sure we get on—and stay on—the loving and right path. He's faithful like that.

Take Sincerity Too Far

Ask the hard question today: Do you want to love others, or do you want to seem like you love others?

70 CONSISTENCY

Jesus Christ is the same yesterday and today and forever.—Hebrews 13:8

In college, I got a degree in religious studies. If that sounds noble or superspiritual, you may never have taken a religious studies course from a secular college. A lot of my classes were interesting and informative—but rarely did they teach me anything about what I believe. I did leave with a broad understanding of other religions, and while the abundance of that kind of knowledge is confusing for some, it always drove me back to Jesus.

But there was this one class on Orthodox Christianity that was full of deeeeep, deep thoughts about God. It's been fifteen years, and I'm still kind of thinking about it. We'd spend weeks just ruminating on these overwhelming ideas about God and how the concepts impacted us, and here's one that always got my little brain working on overdrive: there *are* in fact things God cannot do. (What?! Hold up! Is this heresy?) While He is all-powerful, while He has complete dominion, He cannot *not* be loving. Because then He would cease to be God. And God cannot stop being good, or else He would not be God. God cannot quit being holy, because then He would be inconsistent with His own perfect character.

And the fact that God is infinitely consistent in His character means He is always good. Hebrews 13:8 says it best: Jesus is the same yesterday, today, and forever. He's not changing. He's not going anywhere. (Also included in the crazy theory: God *cannot leave you or forsake you*! Because He's promised He won't, and He can't break promises or else He wouldn't be God!) And He's made you in His image. So if you feel like you're inconsistent or you struggle to be the same day after day, look to His love and grace that have always been coming toward you. Look at His faithfulness that has kept the sun rising since He created it in the first place.

You're made in His image and are growing more like Him by the day. Take it too far, and ask Him to give you a little of His consistency, but also thank Him for the grace that has to catch you if you falter again.

Take Consistency Too Far

If you were going to agree that you're made in the image of God and therefore can behave consistently, what would that look like today? What would you do or say, or how would you allow your presence in the lives of others to make an impact? Ask God to help you do just that.

71 COURAGE

"So do not fear, for I am with you; do not be dismayed, for I am your God. I will strengthen you and help you; I will uphold you with my righteous right hand."—Isaiah 41:10

If I were the enemy and I knew I couldn't actually thwart God's plans for anyone's life, I'd still use fear as a tool to keep them from experiencing abundance. When I think about the really beautiful days of my own life that have been shaded with fear, it makes me sick and tired and done.

Sometimes I'm scared that I'm going to mess up the good and beautiful things He's given me. Sometimes I'm scared they're going to go away. Sometimes I'm even scared about who might be frustrated or put off by my *joy*.

The worst thing is this: fear is not only robbing me of the abundance of my moments; it's also chipping away at my trust in God should something bad come my way. It's stealing joy, and for what? It doesn't make me more prepared for pain in any way, shape, or form.

Lately I sense God calling me to stop playing defense and rather take an offensive stance against fear. I've been feeling that maybe I don't need to spend all my time working against fear, but the true antidote for fear is actually just making courageous and faithful moves. Courage isn't just the absence of fear; for the believer, it's the carrying out of obedient acts fueled by faith that God is who He says He is and will do what He says He'll do.

Let's take our God-given, courageous spirits too far and declare that fear is a liar, our enemy is a thief, and that these are the days of abundance. Let's recognize that fear is not making us any more prepared for potential pain, but rather robbing us of trust, worship, and joy in the moment.

Take Courage Too Far
What would you do if you weren't scared today?
You could move forward and do the courageous
things you feel stirred to do by God.

72 DEVOTION

Devote yourselves to prayer, being watchful and thankful.—Colossians 4:2

Consider this my formal request for a Christian phrase change. I'd like us to scrap the phrase *quiet time* and go back to *devotions*. Let me explain. Today, it's pretty common to hear of someone having a "quiet time," but back when I first came to know Jesus in the late '90s, we called it "devotion time" or "doing your devotions." At least where I grew up, that's what we called the practice of prayer and Bible reading.

My main beef with "quiet time" is this: it's not always that quiet for me. I've got four kids, and for years they were incredibly early risers. If I wanted to be alone in the quiet, I had to get up at around 4 a.m. God may be awake at 4 a.m., but I wasn't really, so I got very used to spending time with God while it was loud around me. I think that worked to my benefit, because now I can go boldly into the throne room of grace while I'm in the car, cooking dinner, in the grocery store, at the gym, in my office, or just about anywhere. I have a high tolerance for noise.

My time alone with God is rarely quiet. I'm talking; He's talking; I might be singing or laughing because I'm just so grateful and overwhelmed by His love for me. It's rarely me sitting quietly under a fuzzy blanket as I stare off sweetly into space.

But "devotion," that's something different. This word *devote* in Colossians 4 is the Greek word *proskartereó*, and it means "to attend constantly, persist, persevere in, continue steadfast in; wait upon." That sounds more like it, am I right? If Jesus is alive and active, and His resurrection power is having its way in and through my life, I don't know how quiet and peaceful my time with Him should look. But to attend to His presence constantly? To persist, persevere, continue steadfastly in, to wait on His Word, attention, affection, and response? Yes—that is an active and faith-fueled stance I can take.

I vote that it's time we kick quiet times to the curb, ask and expect for God to get loud in our lives, and take devotion too far.

Take Devotion Too Far

Pick just one description from the Greek word
proskartereó: "attend constantly," "persist,"
"persevere in," "continue steadfast in," "wait upon."
What would it look like for you to live out your
devotion to Jesus in one of those ways today?

73 CELEBRATION

> On the third day a wedding took place at Cana in Galilee.
> Jesus' mother was there, and Jesus and his disciples had also
> been invited to the wedding. When the wine was gone, Jesus'
> mother said to him, "They have no more wine."—John 2:1–3

Surely one million jokes have been made about Jesus' first miracle being one where He turned water into wine. The story goes like this: Jesus was at a wedding with His mother, Mary. She noticed the bride and groom had run out of wine and instinctively came to Him for help. He basically told her it wasn't His "time" yet (John 2:4 MSG), but Mary still went to the servants and said, "Do what he tells you" (v. 5 ERV). Mary believed what had been spoken to her about her Son and the power He had to shift things.

Jesus merely told the servants to fill some jars with water, He turned the water into wine, and the wedding went on with no one the wiser except for Jesus, Mary, and some servants.

But there are two massive points I want to catch here, both having nothing to do with wine—though I believe there's incredible significance in everything that Jesus does. First, Jesus—with His very limited time on earth and His extreme awareness of the brokenness of the world—made time to go to a wedding. Specifically, He made time to celebrate others.

As we take our jobs and roles very seriously as Christ's ambassadors, as we move throughout our lives and become more and more quickened to the needs and the hurts around us, it's going to become incredibly important that we not neglect time for celebration.

Second, Jesus utilized supernatural power to enhance the celebration, which reminds me that I should not only make *time* to celebrate but also bring intention and passion to it when I do.

The problem arises when we believe that celebration is something we do on our time "off" from God. When we see our jubilees, our parties, as something to keep from Him rather than something to do *with* Him. This may change the way we celebrate, but I also believe it will change the way we work and toil. When we willingly accept moments of celebration into our lives—when we plan for them, bring intention and passion to them—our days will feel less mundane and monotonous, and our worship will feel more alive and real. Celebration is God's idea—let's take it too far, in His ways.

Take Celebration Too Far

Take a moment today to plan some kind of celebration *with* God. Whatever you're celebrating, invite your Father and invite others into your worshipful celebration and thank Him that in the kingdom, celebration is an integral part of our lives.

74 MERCY

> But because of his great love for us, God, who is rich in mercy, made us alive with Christ even when we were dead in transgressions—it is by grace you have been saved.—Ephesians 2:4–5

I was a new lead pastor's wife, and our small church was only a few months old. There were a handful of very wise women who were gathering with us, and heartbreakingly, a large percentage of them had been abused sexually. As I sought to understand their stories, their pain, and how it was currently affecting them, I often heard them talk of God's mercy.

If I'm being totally honest, this attribute of our God was one I'd glossed over in the past. I hadn't thought on it much because it wasn't an attribute I related to. I didn't like needing mercy, and I didn't like giving mercy. Yet these wise and incredible women were showing me with their words and their actions that I needed to perceive it pretty quickly.

The Greek word for mercy in the New Testament is *eleos*, and it means "kindness or goodwill toward the miserable or afflicted, joined with a desire to help them." We might confuse this with pity or even sympathy, which involve feeling sorry for someone—but our all-knowing and kind Father has to take it a step further because He wants His best for us and is pained by our pain. What interests me most about this definition isn't what is included in it, but what's left out. Specifically, it does not seem that mercy rushes us to feel better or to pretend that we do. Mercy does not gloss over pain but goes toward it with help. It does not blame or even seek to teach a lesson. The mercy of God doesn't just feel, and it doesn't just make a plan, but it takes feeling too far by highly valuing action steps that serve the afflicted.

While mercy is not a natural inclination of my flesh, it's an attribute that was purchased for me on the cross of Christ, and because of that I want to take steps to access it daily. More than that, I want to acknowledge how merciful God is toward me when I'm in pain. He's never waiting off to the side, tapping His foot till I get over what has afflicted me. Rather, He's coming toward me in kindness—with hope and healing in His hands.

Take Mercy Too Far

Today, see if you can recall a recent time when
you were in pain either physically or emotionally.
Try to picture how God felt about you, based
on this definition of His mercy. Ask the Holy
Spirit for eyes to see the hurting today.

75 JOY

So celebrate the goodness of God! He shows this kindness to everyone who is his. Go ahead—shout for joy, all you upright ones who want to please him!—Psalm 32:11 TPT

I've heard people talk about choosing joy. But maybe sometimes we have to chase it like we're chasing a sunset, seeing a glimmer of goodness and following the light, regardless of what we were supposed to be doing.

The other night I was driving home from the grocery store with my daughter, and my mind was on all that we had to do when we arrived back at the house. Prep dinner, switch the laundry from washer to dryer, do the whole nighttime routine. But in my peripheral vision, I saw the most brilliant sunset starting to develop—fiery red melting into bright peach in the upper right-hand corner of my front windshield. The left turn onto our street was approaching, but at the last second I stayed the course to go straight.

My daughter and I drove a mile or two north and then pulled into a vacant parking lot to climb on the hood of the car and watch the sunset. We couldn't have chosen that moment by willing it to happen, but we did have to chase it. We had to sense where the joy was coming from and head straight toward it. We had to intentionally set our path to where the warmth of the sun mixed with the atmosphere of our world and brought color.

Maybe sometimes life offers us a choice between joy and sadness. Maybe there are distinguishable moments where it's easy for us to passively accept happy thoughts. But more often I find that I have to direct my soul where to head, I have to chase the signs that God is on the move, I have to get my body aligned with what is happening in the kingdom, and when I get there, joy abounds.

We don't have to work for joy or muster it up, but we might have to follow the signs and run down the path to be in the presence of joy. And this is a gift, our participation in the finding of joy. We don't just get to experience the goodness of God; we get to be active participants in moving toward what He's offered us to bring color and warmth to our lives.

Take Joy Too Far

Today, see if there isn't a small glimmer of joy on the horizon. What would it look like not only to notice it but to chase it? To pull the thread and see what comes from it? What would it look like to thank God for that joyful moment and experience it with Him?

76 AUTHENTICITY

One generation commends your works to another; they tell of your mighty acts. They speak of the glorious splendor of your majesty— and I will meditate on your wonderful works.—PSALM 145:4–5

What in the world does today's verse have to do with authenticity? It's a well-known psalm praising God for His wonderful works. I was reading this passage the other day when it struck me: I want my kids to know how amazing God is. I want to be able to commend God's works to them, to tell of His mighty acts. But most of the ways that God shows up in my life involve my brokenness and often my failure or sin. To tell about some of the amazing things God has done for me, I'm going to have to tell some of the ways I have failed Him. I'll have to be honest about my shortcomings. And, well, that's not super comfortable.

But I thought on it a little longer and realized that more than wanting my kids to grow up and think I'm incredible, I want them to grow up and think that God is incredible. And more than wanting the people in my life to be inspired and blessed by me, I want them to be in awe of God. When I smoosh all these thoughts together, I find that the strength of my praise and proclamation of God's goodness directly correlates with how authentic I am willing to be about my need for Him, His works, His grace, and His goodness. If I don't need God, if I'm okay on my own—then He's not that incredible.

But if I'm desperate for Him, broken and burdened, then His peace and presence and work are transformative, and I'm going to be overwhelmingly and incredibly grateful. What if you're using all your words, time, and efforts to convince the world around you that God is good—but they can't really tell because it seems like you'd be okay without Him? What if what is missing from your testimony and testifying is authenticity? What if that is where the power is?

And as for me and my story, I'd so much rather take authenticity too far, owning up to my need for God and His goodness, than walk around pretending that all is well for the rest of my life.

If the choice is authenticity or pretense, let's follow God's example and in all authenticity allow Him to do His work in our lives, our relationships, and our souls.

Take Authenticity Too Far

When someone asks how you are today, explore the idea of telling the truth. You don't have to air all your dirty laundry or let out the family secrets; just ask the Holy Spirit for a level of authenticity that will create space for you to give some praise to the God who meets you where you are.

77 CONFIDENCE

Now I know, Lord, that you are for me, and I will never
fear what man can do to me.—Psalm 118:6 TPT

Christians (myself included) often get tripped up when it comes to confidence. Are we supposed to be humble or to acknowledge God's power in us? We walk around talking about how we're coheirs with Christ and also boasting that we're the chief of all sinners. It's confusing. But let's not get hypnotized by the complexity, and let's definitely not settle for a watered-down version of humility or confidence just because we're not sure of how they interact with one another. Let's take confidence too far but make sure we're confident of the right things.

Are we supposed to be humble or perceive God's power? What if the two acts are one and the same? What if humility is being confident in God's capacity?

What has God given us? Himself. His power. His character imputed to us as righteousness. His grace. His mercy. His promise to never leave us. We can take confidence too far when we're confident of the character, capacity, and competency of God. And actually, to trust His Word at work in and through our lives, rather than believing in our good works, is a beautiful picture of humility.

Let's settle it once and for all by looking at God's Word—He doesn't want us to walk around with timidity. He doesn't want us to shy away from expecting His power and presence. He doesn't want us to sit still, not making a fuss, pretending we're not quite sure what to do here.

Psalm 118:6 reminds me that I don't have anything to fear, that I can walk in confidence, not because of what I've done for myself—but because of who my Father is.

We should be certain that God does not doubt His own power, and He is not scared He will fail. He is confident, and because we're made in His image, empowered with His Spirit and united with His Son, we can be too.

Take Confidence Too Far

Look first today for a lack of confidence in certain
areas, and then take a moment to capture what that
lack of confidence says about your belief in God.
What has He said about that area of your life?

78 IMPARTIALITY

My brothers and sisters, believers in our glorious Lord Jesus Christ must not show favoritism. Suppose a man comes into your meeting wearing a gold ring and fine clothes, and a poor man in filthy old clothes also comes in. If you show special attention to the man wearing fine clothes and say, "Here's a good seat for you," but say to the poor man, "You stand there" or "Sit on the floor by my feet," have you not discriminated among yourselves and become judges with evil thoughts?—JAMES 2:1–4

Saving seats. That's pretty third grade. We don't do that, right? We're adults here. We don't show favoritism. Except, go with me for a second . . . I've noticed that if I enter almost any church in America these days, there's a pretty defined rubric about who sits where and how important they are based on it. Sometimes we even save whole rows with special placards and nameplates. And I get that while our intention may not be favoritism, that's what it's become. We're people who save seats.

I notice it other places in my life. "I'm too busy to meet with so-and-so, but if so-and-so calls, I can change a few things around." One guest arrives at my party, and I say a casual and warm hello, but when the next human walks in, I jump up and squeal my delight at his or her arrival.

Are any of these impulses inherently sinful? Can we help it if, in our hearts, we prefer certain people to others or have greater affection for different individuals? I think that's up to each of us to take to the Lord and determine, but we can take our actions too far—in the best way—when it comes to honoring, loving, and serving everyone. We can watch our preferences and proclivities and ask the Holy Spirit to steer us toward treating everyone the same. We can look at the example of Jesus and acknowledge that He's given us His capacity to love everyone around us. We can examine the practices of our days and determine if favoritism is present in our lives and take steps toward impartiality powered by the love of God.

Take Impartiality Too Far

See if there is even one rhythm you can shake up
in your life today to be impartial and fair when it
comes to people. Whether it's who you call, who
you serve, who you hug, or who you literally save a
seat for–remember that you're made in the image
of God, and you're not here to play favorites.

79 AFFECTION

"So he got up and went to his father. But while he was still a long way off, his father saw him and was filled with compassion for him; he ran to his son, threw his arms around him and kissed him."—Luke 15:20

I was talking to a young friend the other day about a boy who is interested in her. And like so many women in her age range, she was a little confused and perplexed about his level of affection for her. "He seems so excited to get to date me, which is weird, right? Shouldn't he play it cool?"

I immediately exclaimed, "No! Find a boy who loses his chill over you, and you've made an amazing connection!" I mean, I definitely don't encourage gals to just date the first guy who seems head over heels, but I would encourage most gals I know to pause from moving closer to the guy who seems too cool to express any affection at all.

This is the power play in dating, right? Whoever has the most affection for the other is kind of the weaker member? But these aren't just the games we play in dating; they're also the games we play in other relationships. And I wouldn't be surprised if these messed-up power plays haven't seeped their way into our relationship with God.

The parable of the prodigal son illustrates how our heavenly Father loses all chill when it comes to expressing His feelings for us. But truly?

We don't need a parable; we need only to look at the life, death, and resurrection of Jesus Christ. Our Father sent His only Son, allowed Him to be crucified, and gave Him the authority to be raised from the grave—not because it was good for Him, but so that we could experience the same power that raised Jesus from the dead in our lives.

And He didn't stop there! He also purchased us as ambassadors of His kingdom so we could help others go from darkness to the marvelous light that we now live in. He didn't stop at calling us His servants but instead made us His friends—His coworkers.

God does not keep it cool when it comes to us. So why in the world would we try to keep it cool when it comes to Him? Why would we care more about our earthly dignity than our eternal destiny when it comes to worship and expressing devotion?

Take Affection Too Far

Take a moment today and express your love to God,
full out, without holding back. Turn on a worship song
and take it too far, or journal your praises to Him. Sit
and look at the sky and marvel at what He can do.

80 COMFORT

Praise be to the God and Father of our Lord Jesus Christ, the Father of compassion and the God of all comfort, who comforts us in all our troubles, so that we can comfort those in any trouble with the comfort we ourselves receive from God.—2 Corinthians 1:3–4

I can't get over how much of my life is spent trying to avoid a lack of comfort. I'll go first and confess that I am a girl who likes to feel good. I've had four C-sections and two pretty bad accidents that affected my face, and I truly want to believe that I can avoid ever having a paper cut again. I mean it. No more paper cuts for me. You got that, God?

I want to live a life where it's guaranteed that I won't stub my toe or get in a fight with a friend. I'm terrified of one of my kids getting sick or even my husband having a grouchy mood for a few days. I do not want to encounter pain—not in little ways or big ways. I want to be comfortable.

Yet I live in the world, this big ball of dust, where we exist in the current reality with the belief that eternity is on the way. I live in a place where the difficulties of the fallen world are not off-limits to me. Rather they absolutely can mess with me and alter my day and my life forever. I live in the paradox that God loves me and wants good for me, and that may mean pain passing through His hand toward me, for my good and His glory.

What if taking comfort too far is not about trying to create a world where I never experience anything but joy and good feelings? What if taking comfort too far is instead about facing the inevitable fact that I absolutely will experience pain, and then running to the arms of the Father, who promises comfort in the midst of pain? What if taking comfort too far isn't about trying to secure comfort for ourselves but acknowledging that it's already been secured for us? What if part of the reason that God allows pain in our lives is so that we can perceive and receive His powerful love through His comfort?

I'm going to stub my toe, get a paper cut, experience pain, and watch the people I love do the same at some point in my life. That's probably going to happen at some point today. So rather than trying fruitlessly to create a comfortable life for myself, I'll take it too far and run to the God of all comfort when the unfortunate comes my way.

Take Comfort Too Far

Look for moments when you're trying to avoid pain and instead ask if God will meet you in the midst of it. Thank Him for His presence and ask Him to be powerful in the midst of your discomfort.

81 ADORATION

When one of the Pharisees invited Jesus to have dinner with him,
he went to the Pharisee's house and reclined at the table. A woman
in that town who lived a sinful life learned that Jesus was eating
at the Pharisee's house, so she came there with an alabaster jar of
perfume. As she stood behind him at his feet weeping, she began
to wet his feet with her tears. Then she wiped them with her hair,
kissed them and poured perfume on them.—Luke 7:36–38

I saw something accidentally one day at my sister's house that marked
me forever. I'd come unannounced and slipped in quietly, only to see
something surprising that I wasn't meant to see. I backed away slowly,
with the silhouette of her bent over in prayer burned in my memory for
years to come. She was just praying. In her room. In the middle of the day.
Later I'd surmise that she was praying for God to take away her morning
sickness, because she was in the thick of her first trimester and super sick.
But I walked away thinking, *One day I want to be the kind of woman who
prays on her knees, in the middle of the day, with no one around.*

The unnamed woman in today's scripture, cast aside and cast out by
her society, who washed Jesus' feet—I bet she was the kind of gal who
would have prayed in the middle of the day, on her knees, with no one

watching. She took adoration, worship, and affection for God too far. She wasn't scared to show what she felt, and she wasn't worried anyone would think she was dramatic or too much or emotional or trying to get something from Him.

Isn't it interesting that it's often the women who know the worth of the forgiveness they've received who are willing and able to show their affection in the most radical of ways? It took me years to realize that to be the kind of woman who prayed on her knees, I just needed to be a woman praying. On her knees. There wasn't a badge to hand out or a graduate level of Jesus-loving to reach. I just needed to remember how much He'd done for me and respond accordingly. When we remember what a huge miracle it is that we get to spend time with the God who created the universe, we do it with vigor and passion—and adoration becomes second nature.

Take Adoration Too Far

We can be women who take adoration too far because God has taken His affection and devotion so far for us. We can remember how great His grace is and agree with our lives, our hours, and even our knees that we are the women who are loved by God and who love Him in return.

82 CAREFUL

Cast all your anxiety on him because he cares for you.—1 Peter 5:7

I care. A lot. It comes out the most when I'm trying not to be late. You wouldn't be able to tell from looking at me. I try to do the duck thing—calm on the top, little flipping feet going one hundred miles an hour beneath the surface.

It's not specifically about being late, though that's important to me. I care about how that one person looks at me funny when I walk in the building. Is she upset? Did I forget her birthday? Does she have a headache? Should I go get her some medicine?

I care about what we're eating for dinner next Tuesday. If we have chicken two days in a row, will we get tired of it? Will I forget to get the broccoli again? Should I set a reminder on my phone to thaw the chicken? I know it's not until next Tuesday. I know it will probably be fine. But I care.

Lately, God has begun to show me two things about taking care too far.

1. It's important that I remember that God cares more for me, the details of my life, and the people I love than I ever could. I can't out-care Him. Not with my planning, my stress, or my worrying.

2. God is all-seeing, all-knowing, and all-caring, with a capacity that I can't even fathom. But I have a finite capacity for caring. If I spend all my energy caring about things that may not matter, I will run out of space in my soul and in my brain to care about the things that do matter. So I can learn to be more carefree about being exactly on time to meetings, choosing to show up as on time as possible and care for every human I encounter between now and then.

I can care because God cares for me, and I can live carefree because He cares more than me. But the choice is mine to make wise decisions with the capacity I have to care for myself, my people, and the world around me.

Take Being Careful Too Far

What would it look like for you to take stock today of the things you care about? What increases your mental, emotional, and spiritual capacity to care? What would you do if you accepted the good news that God cares more than you do?

83 NEW LIFE

Therefore, if anyone is in Christ, the new creation has come:
The old has gone, the new is here!—2 CORINTHIANS 5:17

It was the fall of 1999, and I was a fifteen-year-old hot mess. I was far from God and wreaking havoc, lying, and causing trouble for my parents, all while creating a wake of destruction and pain for myself as well.

Until . . .

One fall night, on a retreat, I looked at Jesus and said, "I give up. I give in. You win. Your way is better." Something shifted deep inside me, and I knew I was His. For weeks, months, I'd wake up in the morning and be hit with the realization *God loves me! God is real!* And it was like hearing the good news all over again.

In that season, 2 Corinthians 5:17 was popping up everywhere. For a girl who hadn't paid much attention to Scripture for her entire life, I was suddenly seeing this one Bible verse everywhere. On a journal that a friend gave me, on bumper stickers here and there, in a note from a new friend from church.

The old has gone, the new is here.

I think God knew that even now I'd need the almost-constant reminder that I'm not who I used to be. The conviction, the weight of my present and former sins, was often too much for me to fathom. How had I spent so long running from God? Why did I still do things that didn't honor Him when He'd done so much for me?

The old has gone, the new is here.

When you are in Christ, the five-minutes-ago you has no claim on the five-minutes-from-now you, much less the brokenness and sin from your past. We've each been given a new life, a new identity, a new name, a new history, new gifts, new mercy, and a new standing for the rest of eternity—we have been made new, and we are being made new.

If I'm being honest, I miss the days where that Bible verse lived like a banner in front of my face, and I'd love to bring it back. There must be some correlation between the joy that would hit my heart each morning as I realized that God was real and the frequency with which I was confronted with the truth that I was a new creation.

Those truths in conjunction are what change everything for us: God isn't just good and holy; He's also loving and gracious. He didn't just make us; He's making us new.

Take New Life Too Far

Today, look for a rhythm or pattern from your old life that
needs to go so you can experience the thrill of new life afresh.

84 ABUNDANCE

"I came that they may have life and have it abundantly."—John 10:10 ESV

The night I met Jesus, there was someone preaching, but to be honest, I didn't come to know God through the pastor's words. It was an hour or so later, during a worship session, that I relented and finally submitted my life into Jesus' hands. It felt like submission; it felt like forfeiting a fight. I remember saying something in my head like, *I give up . . . Your way is probably better.* I thought I was losing and exchanging the thrill of my current life for the monotony of a spiritually healthy one. It's funny: I've never had that thought again. Life with Jesus has always been a thrill.

But I do remember some portions of that pastor's message only because they were so silly. He kept talking about abundance, except he called it "a bun dance," and not just because of his extreme Southern accent. He was trying to make it cute, make it into a joke, this extreme sense of muchness that we have access to as believers in Jesus. I'm fairly certain he even had little cartoons of a bun dancing. Again, I don't remember his message but only his repetition of the word, and it's interesting that the spiritual concept of abundance is one that has stuck with me for the last few decades.

Abundance gets confusing for the people of God because we know that we weren't made for more stuff. Most of us know that God is not a genie in a bottle whom we can utilize to produce more money, more material possessions, or more worldly blessings whenever we want. He could do all of those things, and He is the Giver of all the good gifts, but He never promised us comfort, ease, or prosperity in exchange for following Him. Again, at least not from a worldly perspective.

But if God is better than the world's best thing, and if Jesus came that we might have life to the full (see John 10:10), is there a chance that many of us are living on bare-bones spiritual sustenance instead of taking our fill of what He offers? Is there a chance that we've learned to take scraps from the table, maybe even munch off the leftovers of other people's faith, instead of feasting from the fullness that is offered to us from the Creator of the universe?

What does it look like to take abundance too far? Man, I don't know. It feels like the sky isn't even the limit, because we've got a universe of His love, favor, presence, and power to experience. Maybe today is as good a day as any to pause and ask ourselves, *Have I been thinking of life with Christ as losing or giving up instead of gaining and experiencing abundance? Have I been missing out on the thrill of abundance that Jesus purchased for me to have?* Let's take advantage of the abundance, the amazing excess that we have access to.

Take Abundance Too Far

Today, see if you can identify one area in your spiritual life where you've believed you have to just get by instead of experiencing abundance.

85 DIGNITY

> One of the teachers of the law . . . asked him, "Of all the commandments, which is the most important?"
>
> "The most important one," answered Jesus, "is this: 'Hear, O Israel: The Lord our God, the Lord is one. Love the Lord your God with all your heart and with all your soul and with all your mind and with all your strength.' The second is this: 'Love your neighbor as yourself.' There is no commandment greater than these."—MARK 12:28–31

I find the connection between dignity and being dignified so interesting. The dictionary definition of *dignity* is "a sign or token of respect."[3] If you asked most humans who deserves dignity, we'd say everyone. In our minds, especially as believers, we don't want to acknowledge that we qualify people based on their worth or social standing in this world.

But if you look at the definition of *dignify*, you find something that hits closer to home: "to confer honor . . . upon."[4] Whether it's subconscious or realized, we often choose who gets honor in our lives based on a million different variables, and then we treat them better. We give them better seats at the table; we give them more allowances; we stand when they come in the room—even if it's just in our hearts and minds.

But Jesus. In Mark 12 He preached about the greatest commandments—loving God and loving others, and those two in connection with one another can inform and instruct our operations of dignity if we let them. First, if we truly love God—not the God who sounds like us and looks like us, but the One with otherworldly love and care who created the universe and every human in it—I believe we'll want to honor those He made.

Second, if we decide that every human is truly our neighbor, and we heed Jesus' words to love them as much as we love ourselves, dignity will start pouring out of our mouths and hands and hearts. It will start directing our feet and our wallets and informing how we spend our days.

The homeless. The people we don't agree with. Our actual neighbors, the ones who play loud music. If we love God and love our neighbors, we'll hand out dignity and honor—not based on merit or worldly worth—to every human who crosses our path.

Take Dignity Too Far

Ask God to give you eyes for someone you see often but don't treat with dignity. Take it too far in showing that person honor and love, not because it makes you a better person but because Jesus does that for you and me.

86 FERVOR

Be on your guard; stand firm in the faith; be
courageous; be strong.—1 CORINTHIANS 16:13

"Give him favor; give him fervor; guide his steps." This was my prayer
for my husband for years. As he left the house for work or when he walked
up to the front of the church to pray: "Give him favor: God, open doors
for him that only You can. Give him fervor: help him tenaciously take
hold of that which You've taken hold of for him. Guide his steps: be a
lamp to his feet and a light to his path."

It's interesting that in some communities and cultures, fervor is hon-
ored and encouraged, but in others it's kind of discouraged and devalued.
If you act too excited, too passionate, or are too ignited for some cause or
concern, you stand out, and not in a great way.

If our passion is off-putting, should we tone it down? If our excitement
makes others uncomfortable, should we mask it to become more amiable?
When I'm debating whether a God-given attribute is one I want to step
into, it often helps me to consider the antonym. Maybe you can easily name
some synonyms for *fervor*: *intensity, passion, zeal, warmth, ardency*. But what
about those opposite words? Here are a few of the antonyms of *fervor*: *apathy, indifference, insincerity, lethargy, disinterest*, and *dullness*.

I don't know about you, but I'm so thankful that my God is not apathetic or indifferent when it comes to me. I'm so grateful that He is never disinterested or lethargic. Rather, He approaches me, you, and this entire world with passionate fervor. And because we're made in His image, we have access to that same ethos and mind-set.

Let's go forward with passion and purpose, embracing that we've been made fervent because we're His kids. We don't have time for apathy or indifference when our world is hurting and our time is short.

Take Fervor Too Far

Pick one area of your life where you can bring
some fervor today. Show up and take it too far;
bring the passion and leave the passivity at home.
Let the fire of Christ and His kingdom burn
within you till fervor overflows in the best way.

87 CONTENTMENT

The boundary lines have fallen for me in pleasant places;

indeed, I have a beautiful inheritance.—Psalm 16:6 csb

Contentment is such a sweet word. It conjures up thoughts for me of a woman in a comfy sweater, sipping coffee on a fuzzy blanket, with nowhere to go for a few hours. This woman in my head, she seems content. I'm going to be honest: I'm not sure when the last time was that I sat on a sofa in a comfy sweater with a cozy blanket and nowhere to go. I'm not even sure where this picture came from, but I think it's time to throw it out the window.

In comparison, most of my days are full, there is often a coffee stain on my shirt, and on the rare occasion that I don't have somewhere to go, one of my four kids does. But honestly, I can access contentment right where I am; I just may need to change the language I use for it and the picture of what it looks like.

Contentment does not come when we're finally sitting or when we get what we think we want. Contentment does not come passively or by osmosis, and I actually don't think it's a soft word or a sweet action step but rather an active choice, an empowered declaration. Contentment is a fighting stance.

The woman who chooses contentment by the power of the Holy Spirit is the one who refuses to let her circumstances dictate her joy. The woman who chooses contentment is the one who looks at her life with spiritual eyes and eternal expectancy. The woman who chooses contentment is the gal who moves forward boldly believing in God's love and abundant goodness—no matter what she's wearing, where she's sitting, who she's with, or how much is on her plate. She knows that Jesus is the prize, contentment is hers for the choosing, and abundance is here.

Take Contentment Too Far

Today, take contentment too far by refusing to wait
for it to come; instead, actively choose it. Declare
how God has drawn pleasant lines for you, and speak
life and hope and possibility over some circumstance
that the enemy might want you to discount.

88 CREATIVITY

God spoke: "Let us make human beings in our image."—Genesis 1:27 MSG

My friend April may be the most creative person I know. From the moment I met her, her life has oozed color and vibrancy, passion and purpose. She dresses creatively, she makes art that is creative, and she even loves creatively. She's also kind and sweet and would never hurt a fly, but if you want to see her get angry, there is one surefire way to do it: tell her that *you're* not creative.

I'll admit, when I first met her, I made this horrible mistake. I told April I wasn't creative once when we were hanging out, she rebuked me, and a few months later I started an art business—selling designs that incorporated Scripture. That print shop changed my life and my family's lives. It's enabled us to support multiple employees and fund church plants and adoptions all over the world, and now we've got art in thousands and thousands of homes on multiple continents. I'm so glad April told me to stop saying I wasn't creative.

Her simple argument was this: "If you're made in the image of God, you're creative. He did not hold back or hold out on you when it came to any of His attributes—so don't limit what He can do through you."

I'm not just glad I listened to April so I could start the print shop, but I'm glad I repented of that false belief that I wasn't creative so I could experience more of God in multiple areas of my life. I've gotten to commune with Him, create with Him, and see His Spirit move in ways I never would have if I'd kept walking around saying I wasn't creative.

I've been able to bring creativity into my problem-solving, my parenting, my ministry, and even the way I handle "boring" logistical things like figuring out a carpool schedule. Partnering with creativity pushes me to come to the table expecting to see color and abundance. Trusting in God's creativity and His power in and through me makes me excited for life, excited for what's next, excited to grow.

You, friend, are creative—because you're made in the image of God. What if you could move from denying that fact about yourself to taking it too far and even celebrating it in just one day? I think you can, because I know He can.

Take Creativity Too Far

See if you can pick just one area of your life that feels gray, drab, and devoid of creativity. Ask God to surprise you by acting creatively. He can move wherever He wants, and He can bring color to any space.

89 TRUST

Those who trust in the LORD are like Mount Zion, which
cannot be shaken but endures forever.—PSALM 125:1

This past spring our family went to Yosemite, which was thrilling and so
different from our normal landscape since we live on the East Coast, near
the beach. I did all kinds of research on our travel out there—looking
up the best hikes, trails, and coffee shops, because I've got my priorities
straight.

I found a trail that looked beautiful and was hikeable for my kiddos,
and I started googling all sorts of information about that particular hike
so I could know all there was to know. You can imagine my shock when
I found on one Google search that the hike we were about to embark on
was literally the one where the most people have died at Yosemite. Say
what? Why do they suggest this for little kids? Why are we going there?
More research showed me that it wasn't that the hike itself was perilous
but that the waterfall nearby was deceptively deadly. It looked calm from
the outside but could be dangerous for people who stuck their feet in.

We were almost to the trailhead when I read this crucial information,
so I kept the facts to myself but gave my kids a stern lecture on *staying
on dry ground*. No feet in the water, friends! Don't even look at the water!

It wasn't until we were well into the hike, and I was basically a stress basket case, that I realized my relationship with trust is a lot like that waterfall. It feels deceptively enticing to dip my toe into the waters of stress and fear, it feels comforting to worry about something (as if it will help), until I realize that I've slowly slipped backward into a lack of trust.

Let's take it too far, this idea of trust, shall we? Often when I'm struggling with understanding a principle, I'll do this thing where I reverse the scripture to see what it would be like if I didn't believe it. Let's take Psalm 125:1 and write the opposite of it: Those who don't trust in God are like little ant hills; they live frazzled and shaken, and they don't last very long.

Woosh! Okay. I hear You, God. I want to take trusting Him too far. I want it to be said of me that I actively believed in God and His goodness.

Take Trust Too Far
See if there are any areas of your life where you've dipped your toe into the waters of fear versus trust. Is there any place that you're choosing worrying and striving over resting and believing?

90 CONFESSION

Lord, you have searched me and known me.—Psalm 139:1 CSB

It took me a while to understand that whether or not I acknowledge it, whether or not I know it, whether or not I like it, I am intimately known by God.

When we don't have a choice about whether to be known by a human, that's not great. That's called stalking. Stalkers are nothing to joke around about. Seriously. As it pertains to privacy and people prying into my life at any level, I can honestly be a little paranoid. I've watched a handful of made-for-TV movies about stalkers, and I've seen enough news stories to know it's not cool when someone is in your space when you don't want him or her to be. Stalkers don't have our consent to be in our lives.

On the other hand, it's the willing consent, the surrender to being known, that makes getting to know people an enjoyable process for us. That's when being known becomes being friends. And that's partially why I think God allows us to experience the thrill of confession.

Think about it: when we do something wrong, when we stray from believing and living in alignment with who God has made us to be—He knows. No matter what, He's aware. In fact, He knows before we do wrong; He knows even if no one else does. He knows the sin that is as small as a fleeting thought and as deep as the darkest buried secret we could ever imagine.

Yet He gives us the gift of compassion and the capacity to confess to Him—to willingly acknowledge what it is that we have or haven't done. Why? Because He knows that hiding produces shame, and shame typically leads to more sin, doubt, and discouragement.

Confession breaks the chains of silence and puts defeat, discouragement, and condemnation to bed. Confession leads to repentance, which leads to refreshment, which is where we experience kindness, which leads to life change. Confession is His gift to us, to allow us a part of the process—so we aren't just found out, but we get to grow and shift from our mistakes. We aren't just made known by God; we're given tools to continually, willingly expose our hearts to His grace and to His love . . . because it's good for us.

Take Confession Too Far

Take confession too far today and open up
to God about something, anything. You
won't leave the same, but I bet you will leave
feeling loved and seen in the best way.

91 FUN

So I commend the enjoyment of life, because there is nothing better for a person under the sun than to eat and drink and be glad. Then joy will accompany them in their toil all the days of the life God has given them under the sun.—Ecclesiastes 8:15

Everybody has a Bible verse or a story or a set of scriptures that trips them up. Maybe you have one that's hard for you to understand; maybe it's difficult to comprehend and reconcile with what you know of God. Mine may be surprising: Ecclesiastes, man. It messes me up every time. Over and over again.

I am an achiever. I am a worker. I am a scheduler. I am a woman on mission. I often say that I don't want to put up curtains in a house that's burning down. Since I met Jesus, I just want to tell as many people about Him as possible so they can experience His abundance on earth and go to heaven too. Absolutely I love fun, but productive fun. Fun as we're going. Fun on the way to changing the world.

I was traveling with my assistant recently, and someone asked if we hang out outside of work. I said no, and that's when my assistant noted, "Jess doesn't really hang out with *anyone* outside of work, church, or mission—she just hangs out with them during it." Which is absolutely true, because I don't naturally want to spend my time on things that don't help the mission of God go forward. If I'm being honest, I've found that even my rest is a means to an end. I just rest so I can work hard again. I take rest seriously because I don't want to burn out.

But here's what I've found: when I stop making time for fun—pure fun for fun's sake—it's because I've forgotten that God loves me enough to let me enjoy life. I've forgotten that I am His personal treasure, not a tool He uses to get stuff done. I've forgotten that He loves to see me smile.

So I keep reading Ecclesiastes, and I keep planning fun things. Because I can take even this too far, this experiencing God through the pure enjoyment of life. He's in the fun, He's around the fun, and I know Him better when I surrender to it.

Take Fun Too Far

Take five minutes–or fifty–and have fun today. Dance with your kids; laugh with your friends; watch a silly YouTube video about cats. Go to an arcade or go on a walk. Whatever you do, believe that God loves you enough to let you enjoy Him without getting ahead.

92 FAIRNESS

> Peter turned and saw that the disciple whom Jesus loved was
> following them. (This was the one who had leaned back against
> Jesus at the supper and had said, "Lord, who is going to betray
> you?") When Peter saw him, he asked, "Lord, what about him?"
> Jesus answered, "If I want him to remain alive until I return,
> what is that to you? You must follow me."—John 21:20–22

This may be one of my top ten favorite passages in the Bible.

First, let's start with the big stuff. In this chapter of John, *resurrected Jesus is making Peter breakfast*. Peter, the very friend and disciple who has betrayed Him three times is now being greeted with open arms, miraculous catches of fish, and a breakfast made by the Savior of the world. This is some crazy stuff.

The whole chapter is chock-full of Peter and Jesus having some important talks, but then Peter shows his true colors by worrying about what's going to happen with someone else. And Jesus comes back with the ultimate, "You get what you get, and you don't throw a fit."

That's the line I use when my kids are bickering about something that doesn't seem fair to them. It's hard to explain to children that fair might not be equal, and we may not get what others do, but we always get God's best. Because what's the alternative: believing that God holds out on some of us? No thanks.

But how can we take this picture of Jesus' fairness and make it so that we are fair to others? I think we do exactly what Jesus did: we throw equal and balanced out the window, and we treat everyone with God's best.

It's interesting how the idea of abundance squashes fairness. If you always give everyone what you can for God's best to come forth in their lives, fair goes out the window. Because everyone is different, and what He wants for them varies. But if we make it our mission to be the kids of His that want His abundance, His best, and His good gifts for all His other kids around us, we'll always end up treating others fairly, even if it doesn't look balanced.

Here's to being fair people, to being women who don't check to make sure everyone is being fair with us in return but rather expect that God's best is coming toward us and He'd never hold out.

Take Fairness Too Far

Ask God to show you ways He's been gracious and blessed you, throwing the scales of fairness and balance away with His mercy and love. Ask Him for one way you can lavish someone else with love and blessing today.

93 PRAYER

The LORD is near to all who call on him, to all who call on him in truth. He fulfills the desires of those who fear him; he hears their cry and saves them.—PSALM 145:18–19

Do you have a Jesus voice? You know what I'm talking about. Most people have a cadence, a distinction that occurs in their speaking voice when they're praying in public. You can find awesome memes online that poke fun at some of the ways we pray, such as the number of times we repeat, "Father God," like we're talking to some foreign dignitary.

Something like this: *"Father God, we thank You, Father God, for this day, Father God, and oh, Father God, we ask forgiveness, Father God . . ."*

I first noticed the use of "the Jesus voice" when I met a contemporary in college whose voice was not even slightly different when she spoke to God in public. She just started talking to Him like she talked to me, and it marked me.

So for a handful of years after that, I watched my own voice and tried to talk to God as if He were physically with me—with reverence, but with my real, natural voice, the one I'd use to speak with a friend. I also tried to use everyday words. Sometimes when I'd pray, I'd say something like, "Hey. I'm tired. Will You help me wake up? I don't want to fall asleep reading the Bible today." Or I'd say, "Today was pretty discouraging. I wasn't expecting that. Will You help me see what You're up to here? I want to be on the same page as You."

But eventually I got insecure about my honest prayers, especially in front of others who used such a distinguished "Jesus voice," and I worried that maybe I wasn't treating God with enough reverence. So I asked my friend who is a Bible scholar to weigh in; was I missing something? Is there anything in the Word that speaks to us being specifically polite or using solemn words when approaching the throne room of grace?

And here's what she told me: If God is truly our good Father and also our friend, we ought to consider how we speak to that friend when meeting with Him. Is it polite to use fake words that we don't really mean? No. Is it polite to talk the whole time and not listen? No. Is it polite to say His name repetitively, like we don't really have true intimacy with Him? No. So even if we want to be polite, the most loving thing we can do is to say honest and true words. To just talk to God as if He's our Father and Friend and Counselor, which He has established Himself to be.

Take Prayer Too Far

Talk to God today. With your real voice. Out loud. Tell Him
what you think, what you feel, what you want, what you need.
Take a few moments to listen and see where He leads.

94 HOPE

> Therefore, since we have been justified through faith, we have peace with God through our Lord Jesus Christ, through whom we have gained access by faith into this grace in which we now stand. And we boast in the hope of the glory of God. Not only so, but we also glory in our sufferings, because we know that suffering produces perseverance; perseverance, character; and character, hope. And hope does not put us to shame, because God's love has been poured out into our hearts through the Holy Spirit, who has been given to us.—Romans 5:1–5

I have one sentence of this passage memorized, and it's the most memorable and maybe the easiest to take out of context: "And hope does not put us to shame."

If I'm praying for a friend whose mom is sick, I might pray that God would get our hopes up, since hope doesn't put us to shame. If one of my kiddos has a hard test coming up, I will pray for wisdom and clarity for him or her and then speak this truth over both of us: we can hope for the best because hope doesn't put us to shame. But it's the earlier part of the passage that really unpacks *why* we can so vehemently agree with this truth.

We boast in the *hope of the glory of God*. It's not hope that everything will turn out the way we want it to. It's not hope that we'll get all we ever wanted. It's hope that heaven will come to earth, that the kingdom of God will advance, that God will get more glory—and *that* can happen in good circumstances, and it can certainly occur in hard ones.

Sure, we've got a preference. Sure, we've got a potential unfolding of the scenario that is more favorable from our perspective—but we are free to hope, safe to hope, because ultimately, we already have the prize. We already have God, admittance into His family, and the strength of the knowledge of truth that He's got us, He loves us, He wants good for us, and He does good for us.

We can take it too far with hope. We can get our hopes up. It's not the outcome that will hold us, keep us, carry us—but God is big enough for us to tell Him our preferences. We know that at the end of the day, we walk away with Him. We get the prize because we're in the kingdom, and we're His girls.

Take Hope Too Far

See if there's one area where you've lost hope. Today, take some time to write down your preferences, your best-case scenario in that area. Ask God to help you get your hopes up, and ask Him to help you remember that He's the prize.

95 FINISHING

So now finish doing it as well, so that your readiness in desiring it may be
matched by your completing it out of what you have.—2 CORINTHIANS 8:11 ESV

A few years ago, I moved from one house to another. I hate moving.
I hate moving alone, but moving with four kids and a dog—*blerg*. It's
the worst. But having a house is a blessing, and I believe that God is in
transitions, so I was trying not to complain and instead to be grateful,
even though *I hate moving.* And listen: I come by it honestly. We moved
ten times in our first nine years of marriage, and I had a happy heart
through most of those moves—but now I just feel like all my tolerance
for the idea has worn off.

The day of the big move, we had a dozen or so friends over to help
us, which was such a blessing. And as we were finishing loading up at the
old house, preparing to drive a few blocks to the new house, I just kind
of lost it. I was walking with my friend Kristen, taking a step away to
blink back some tears because I was just so exhausted, when I said, "I'm
not good at finishing. I hate finishing. I love starting. I just don't want
to finish this move."

Kristen wasn't at all trying to be discouraging when she said, "The
good news is you're only at the beginning of moving, really. This is

just the first part. So you don't have to worry that you're not good at finishing!"

There are those of us who have believed that we're not good finishers, that we'll never see the end, that we'll never make it to the final curtain, because we've forgotten that we're made in the image of God. He is good at both beginnings and endings, and He's equipped us with what we need to cross the finish line, no matter which point we find ourselves at on the journey.

And what's even more beautiful is that He is always making everything new, so even when it feels like we're at the ending of something—it's always a beginning. When it comes to eternity and final things, this is truly just the first part, and we can expect God's abundance and power and presence in all the seasons.

Take Finishing Too Far

Is there an area of your life where you don't believe
you can finish well? Take some time today to thank
God that He is not only the starter but the ultimate
finisher, and ask Him for guidance on how you
can finish well–empowered by His strength.

96 GENEROSITY

As Jesus looked up, he saw the rich putting their gifts into the temple treasury. He also saw a poor widow put in two very small copper coins. "Truly I tell you," he said, "this poor widow has put in more than all the others. All these people gave their gifts out of their wealth; but she out of her poverty put in all she had to live on."—LUKE 21:1–4

Every week, sometimes multiple times per week, I see a modern-day depiction of the widow's mite lived out. I've got to tell you about Belle. Belle is a sweet, wild (in the best ways) high school student who goes to our church and who also happens to be a spectacular babysitter. She wears a beret and a smile that's bigger than you can imagine. She's bright and sunny and kind, and she is one of the most cheerful and faithful givers I've ever met.

How do I know? Venmo. We've got a young church, with lots of high schoolers and college students, and we realized that they rarely carried cash and hardly any had checkbooks, so to help them tithe, we had to let them use the Venmo app—where you can easily transfer money from friend to friend electronically. It's been cool to see a lot of them start using it, but no one is as faithful as Belle. I can always tell when she's been babysitting because I'll see $3 or $4 pop up in the app.

One time she babysat for me, and before her car left my driveway, I saw the little notification pop up on our church's Venmo. Belle had tithed! Of course! Because she is generous and God has been generous with her.

Nothing defeats the work of the enemy in our lives quite like taking generosity too far. It fights defeat; it fights the lie or the feeling that we don't have enough or that God hasn't done good for us. It declares that I have *more* than enough, and I know God will continue to provide for me.

Taking generosity too far fights fear with the belief that more is on the way. It fights the fear of missing out, because often our money goes where we cannot. Taking generosity too far is worshipful, and it's important that we remember it doesn't matter how much we give but rather that we approach giving with belief in God's ability, not our own, to take care of us.

Take Generosity Too Far

Instead of thinking how little you have to give (time, money, energy, anything), ask God today to show you what you can willingly give with a cheerful heart because He's been so generous with you.

97 FREEDOM

It is for freedom that you have been set free.—Galatians 5:1 paraphrased

This passage in particular is speaking to the spiritual freedom we have—the release we have from the burden of unforgiven sin. I love kind of quirky Bible verses. And while everyone loves to quote Galatians 5:1, I happen to think it's pretty quirky. "It is for freedom that you have been set free." This to me sounds like you're saying, "It's for waffles that you eat waffles." Or, "It is for trees that we have trees." Or even an abstract one: "It is for celebration that we celebrate."

But it does start to make sense when we look more closely at the wording. For instance, it *could* say that it's for some other purpose that we've been set free. Like, "It's for the good of others that you've been set free" or "It's for your finances that you've been set free." But no, God says it is for freedom that we've been set free, which means that freedom alone is worth setting someone free.

Let's think about it like this: I don't just go to the dentist because going to the dentist is where the fun is. I go because it helps me keep my teeth healthy. I don't just go to the grocery store because I love walking the aisle. I go there because we need food and I have to feed my family.

But unlike going to the dentist or the grocery store, to experience freedom doesn't require a reason. It was worth enough to Jesus Christ to pay the price for us to merely experience it. And it doesn't *have* to produce anything else to have fulfilled its purpose. He didn't purchase freedom for us so that we can be better leaders. He didn't need us to be free so we could work harder or preach better or get our lives tidied up. He just wanted us to experience the exhilaration of living in liberty because that's who He created us to be. Our freedom alone was worth the cost; it didn't have to be a package deal with any other add-ons.

And, of course, it's that lavish love that motivates us, compels us to actually want to take our freedom and move forward in obedience. It's our sense of freedom that keeps us coming back to Jesus, not because we have to—but because we get to. It's obtaining our freedom that makes us want to share the good news of Jesus Christ. Because when you have something this good, the only natural response is to share it.

Take Freedom Too Far
Is there a burden or an expectation that you've placed
on yourself or allowed the world to place on you that
God never did? Throw it off today, in Jesus' name,
and celebrate that liberty you've been given.

98 FIGHTING

Fight the good fight of the faith. Take hold of the eternal life to which you were called when you made your good confession in the presence of many witnesses.—1 Timothy 6:12

My daughter was really sick once, and she had to be taken by ambulance to the emergency room. We had rushed out of our home so early that morning that I hadn't brushed my teeth, and when my mom and sister arrived from two hours away, they found me brushing my teeth in my daughter's emergency room.

She was still critically ill, and would be for some time, so you can imagine their shock when they found me, not by her bed, not crying or praying, but standing over the sink, brushing my teeth and quietly staring off into space. Gently, my mom asked for details and updates, and then pulled me aside and said some of the most loving words I've ever heard her say: *"You're going to have to fight."*

Mom coached me through asking about medications and different treatment options and fighting spiritually—she reminded me that this tragedy was not just happening to us without any options to respond. We could pray; we could call others to pray; we could worship; we could fight.

Our daughter lived, and God miraculously spared her body through a few years of battling that illness, but it marked me and shifted the way I approach everyday life, as you can imagine.

A few years later, I got a message from someone asking me why I always used such violent language when it came to my walk with God. Why did I talk about battles and fighting and warring in the spirit? Couldn't faith be more about resting in God's work?

I immediately thought about my daughter and her time being sick. I thought about how God could have accomplished anything He wanted whether I prayed or not. I thought about all the times I've done battle in the spiritu, praying for something that *didn't* go the way I'd hoped or planned. And I realized that God can do it all without our participation, but I'm so glad He doesn't.

Take Fighting Too Far
Read 4 Timothy in its entirety today, and remember who God has made you to be.

99 CHARACTER

"For there is nothing hidden that will not be disclosed, and nothing concealed that will not be known or brought out into the open."—Luke 8:17

I once dreamed I had a terrifying box of bones hidden in the closet. That dream got me, because for so long the body was outside of my house. This time it had moved in closer. As the dream with the bones in the closet progressed, I got more and more anxious because I could tell (in the dream) that my husband was going to look for something in the closet. I obviously didn't want him to find my secret. But the dream ended with him on a stepstool, reaching in and then handing me a diamond, still never seeing the bag of bones I'd been keeping from him. I woke up pretty shaken and then called and asked a friend if she had any interpretation for me.

"We won't even be able to enjoy the gifts God is giving us if we're hiding secret sin, Jess. Maybe you used to feel like your sin was removed from you—far from you—but it's not. It's intimately positioned in your life, especially when you're hiding it."

I knew I hadn't committed murder. I wasn't struggling with any addictions or life-altering secrets. But I did have some current temptations and indulgences that I would have considered "baby sins." And I was definitely hiding them.

You can step into wonderful moments, receiving gifts from God left and right, even when you're dealing with secret bits of sin. But! You might just not enjoy those moments as much as you would if you brought everything into the light. Abundant life with Jesus is like the world's biggest and best diamond. Let go of your "bones" and reach for that diamond instead.

The only human who had perfect character was Jesus, and He's not asking any of us to be perfect. He is, however, constantly offering us the grace and goodness of His mercy—the chance to take good character too far by bringing things we've hidden in the darkness into the light and letting His love and redemption shine on them. Because we've got closets and closets full of diamonds, and He's already paid the price for every single bag of bones that we think we need to hide.

Take Character Too Far

Confess one thing to Jesus today that He already knows but that you've been trying to hide from Him. Thank Him for His grace and mercy and forgiveness and ask Him if there's anything He'd have you do to walk in the light fully.

100 DEPENDENCE

Hear me, LORD, and answer me, for I am poor and needy.—PSALM 86:1

We value independence so much these days. And I get it, because I value independence myself. We romanticize going out on our own and doing wild and wonderful things by ourselves, which is definitely not a bad thing, but something to note.

It's also worth noting that at some point in life, we begin to villainize dependence. We say the phrase "still living at home with my parents" as if it's a death sentence, and potentially one of the most insulting words we can call a person in our current culture is *needy*. "Oh, she's so needy!" "He's a nice guy and all but he's super needy—he wanted to talk on the phone every day."

When did it become such an insulting and vile thing to acknowledge your needs, ask for them, and even live into them? When did independence become the ultimate goal in life? It's especially disconcerting when so much of God's Word speaks to our need for Him. We need Him for life, for breath, for wisdom, for connection. We need Him for growth, for gifts, for vision, for insight. We need the blood of Jesus for salvation, for redemption, for freedom, and for healing. We need the Holy Spirit for power, for comfort, for unity, and for change. We need

God. Yet in every other area of our lives we're taught that it's best if we don't need anyone or anything.

It begs the questions, Are we really all that independent outside of our relationship with God? Is it truly healthy to move about in the world never needing anyone or craving their presence?

Here's what I've found: When I throw off my desire to be totally independent and instead go boldly into the throne room of grace, asking God for all that He's got, I take most of what I need straight from the Source. My encouragement, my comfort, my wisdom, my vision, my help—it all comes from God. And then I'm in a better place to walk with other humans in a more balanced way. I'm ready to share with them, but I'm also humbled and eager to be blessed and to receive from them as well.

Let's take our dependence on God too far, throwing off the lie the world tells us about never needing anyone. He's our Father, and He longs to meet us right where we are with exactly what we need.

Take Dependence Too Far
Talk to God today and identify three things you need
from Him. Ask for help, and see how your day shifts.

NOTES

1. Dictionary.com, s.v. "self-righteous," accessed July 1, 2019, https://www .dictionary.com/browse/self-righteous.
2. Merriam-Webster.com, s.v. "righteousness," accessed July 1, 2019, https://www.merriam-webster.com/dictionary/righteous.
3. Dictionary.com, s.v. "dignity," accessed July 8, 2019, https://www .dictionary.com/browse/dignities.
4. Dictionary.com, s.v. "dignify," accessed July 8, 2019, https://www .dictionary.com/browse/dignify?s=t.

ABOUT THE AUTHOR

Jess Connolly is a gal who is in the thick of it herself. She is the author of *Dance, Stand, Run* and *You Are the Girl for the Job*, and coauthor of *Wild and Free* and *Always Enough, Never Too Much*. She is also the co-owner of All Good Things Collective print shop and helped start both She Reads Truth and The Influence Network. She and her husband planted Bright City Church in Charleston, South Carolina, where they live with their four children. She blogs at jessconnolly.com.